Designing Interviews

(for the hiring manager)

First edition. Published by Sternly Worded, San Francisco, CA, USA

ISBN 979-8-9987385-9-3

Cover and text design by Josh Silverman.

Body serif typeface: Brix Slab. Body and header sans typeface: Koga Sans.

Illustrations by Betsy Streeter.

Contents

Foreword

Jared Spool

Maker of Awesomeness, Center Centre

As a design manager, hiring is the most important thing you'll ever do. Get it right, and you will build a fantastic team of exceptionally competent people. The rest of your management will be a breeze, because the team you'll end up putting together will work seamlessly together. Your team will deliver results that will become the envy of every manager in your organization.

However, if you get the hiring wrong, it has enormous consequences. I've found that failures in hiring fall into two categories: bad and much worse.

Bad hiring failure: You lose a candidate who would've become a great addition to your team. Pushing a candidate away means hiring takes longer. Hiring is disruptive enough. Extending it unnecessarily by days or weeks is costly. It hurts morale and, in some cases, damages your team's reputation.

Much worse hiring failure: You hire a candidate who is not right for your team. Now, you have more considerable management challenges, as you try to figure out if you can somehow magically transform them into someone close to what you need. Or, if you can't (the more likely outcome), go through the process of letting them go (and all the work and issues that entails) and then starting the process again to find the person you should've hired originally.

Over my career, I've hired hundreds of people, and I used to think it was a factor of luck that a team member would work out. I now believe differently. After I started using the techniques that led to great hiring, which these pages so wonderfully describe, I saw a dramatic increase in the quality of the teams I built.

Yet, you'll be hard pressed to find another book discussing what it takes to hire design team members. And our design communities have almost no discussion about the practices that lead to building great teams.

In these pages, Margo guides you through the process. First, you must define the position – a critical step many hiring managers skip, and pay the price for later. Then you need to craft an ad that carefully attracts the right person. Then you need a fast and efficient interview process.

After you find the ideal candidate, you want to get them to an offer quickly, but not until you've thoroughly vetted them to ensure you haven't missed something that could make things painful down the road. Be efficient but not at the expense of quality.

That's why I'm so excited about this book. I'm even more excited that you've decided to give it a read. Our field needs more high-power design teams to show the world what top-quality design can do.

And it all starts by hiring the right person for your next opening.

P.S. While you're at it, flip the book over and give the other side a read. As a design professional, you should understand what the 'user experience' is like.

Margo has done an excellent job delivering sound guidance on how to smooth the rails when trying to get hired. You can make it even better by designing a hiring process that takes the candidate's needs into account. Which will get you even better candidates, and eventually, a great team.

CHAPTER ONE

Designing the design job

First of all, well done. You've gone through the hurdles to actually open up a spot on your team. Or someone left. Or you had to let someone go. OK, maybe the congrats was too early. But no matter the reason you're here, you're here! You get to bring someone onto your team. You're a job creator. You should run for president.

Maybe we're getting ahead of ourselves.

Setting out to bring someone new onto your team isn't as simple as putting a #hiring! badge on your LinkedIn profile. Hiring is work. Filling a job is a job. You're likely to spend hours sifting through resumes and portfolios, conducting interviews and collecting feedback from hiring panels. There's a lot to do. So how can you make sure you're sifting through the right resumes, talking to the right candidates, and conducting the right interviews?

I'll tell you this: you don't want to just start with a job description.

Before the search begins

When I first started conducting interviews for this book, I had the absolute privilege to have a chat with Jared Spool. Jared is a legend in the UX community: he's known for being an expert in the fields of usability, technology, design and all things UX, specifically hiring and building high-functioning UX teams. Suppressing a great deal of imposter syndrome, I sent him early chapters and an outline. I was open to any and all advice, and I couldn't wait to hear what he had to say.

"Great managers hire people who are actually really capable to do the work. Poor managers hire people who are often not capable to do the work. They don't do enough upfront work, and unfortunately, the early draft of your book reflects that flaw."

<gulp>. "Tell me more," I said.

"So you have the job description as the first thing you do, right?"

"Right."

"Yeah, for us in our work, it's the fourth or fifth document I have people produce. I need them to *design the position* long before they write the job description. To me, writing the job description is going straight to code."

Oof, this felt like a lot. Four or five documents? What could they be? This sounded like a lot of work. A lot of work to write a chapter about, let alone do. But the more I heard Jared's explanation, the more I understood that this aligned perfectly with my point-of-view: hiring isn't about going on vibes or ticking off a list of required skills. It's about systematically understanding the role and the comparable skills needed to be successful at it, then making that match with the right candidate. It's about being strategic, efficient, and building relationships with the people who will work with this new hire. It's not about taking it all on yourself as the hiring manager and just going with your gut.

I'll go through what Jared shared with me. What he acknowledges he adapted from Lou Adler, author of *Hire with your Head: Using Performance Based Hiring to Build Great Teams*. (Hot tip: when you Google said author, make sure to add "hiring" to your search term or you'll end up learning too much about the record producer.) I am calling it "The Jared Method™."

It looks like this:

The Thank-You Note. An imaginary thank-you note to your new hire on their 1-year anniversary that will inform how you design the job.

The Performance Profile. An exhaustive doc that lists all the accomplishments this person would have done in their first year and the skills they demonstrated to do all that stuff.

The Have/Learn Table. A document that lists those skills to see if candidates have them, or have the capacity to learn them.

The Assessment Criteria. A checklist of all the evidence you need to see from each candidate, and a way to score them, from basic to distinguished.

Please do not run away. I know. I KNOW this seems like a lot of work to do even before you post that fancy new job description that's burning a hole in your Google Docs. But here's the thing: the time you spend designing the position is time you will save screening, interviewing, and assessing candidates that are not right for the job. The time you spend making the right hire is the time you'll save coaching and correcting the wrong hire. Beyond saving time, you'll save yourself and that wrong candidate a lot of heartbreak.

And I know you care about improving the way you hire. After all, you have this book in your hand (thank you, btw).

Beyond just making your hiring process more effective, more efficient, and with better-performing hires, going through this process will get crucial buy-in from the other people you work with. As we'll talk about in later chapters, hiring is not a solo sport, and you'll need those folks aligned and working with you, every step of the way.

The Thank-You Note

Imagine it is not today, but a year from now. Your new hire is so good at their job. Colleagues pass you in the halls and say, "Good hire." When it comes to allocation time, quite a few teams are vying for their time. You're proud of them. You're proud of yourself a bit too. So let's write the new hire a thank-you note, letting them know specifically why everyone nods and smiles when someone mentions their name.

In this note, you'll focus on two things:

Accomplishments. Accomplishments cover everything they did: they onboarded quickly, they got right to work solving a specific problem while leveraging particular skills. They built key relationships with key people, grew the team, improved a certain skillset for other people, or implemented a whole new way of working. Be exhaustive, dream big. What are all the things your ideal candidate could achieve?

Benefits. Now, for each of these accomplishments, cover the benefits that came as a result. Why was onboarding quickly important? What problem did they solve or feature did they help develop, and what was the impact on the business. Now that the team has that new skillset, what have they been able to do? What did this awesome new hire unlock in the cross-functional team, in their peers, for you as their manager? Be exhaustive, dream big! How are all the ways the business feels a positive impact as a result of this hire?

Once the Thank-You Note is written, circulate it to the people who are stakeholders for this job. This might look like the people you'd like on the hiring panel, the people they'll be working with, the people who approved the headcount in the first place. Ask for their feedback, give them all the commenting rights. This helps them really understand what you've envisioned the role to be and plants the seed for how they should assess candidates.

Jared said, "I remember having a position that I had talked about in meetings. Oh, we should get a person who does this. I kept calling them a 'journalist.' And people kept nodding their heads yes and no or yes and yes. 'That sounds great, whatever you say. Jared, fine'. But when I wrote up the Thank-You Note and I circulated it, I got comments back like 'You've been talking about this for four months, and I finally now understand what you are looking for. And here's my feedback.'"

The Thank-You Note allows you to both sketch out the job, but also get actionable feedback on the true role, responsibilities and capacities of this particular person. It gets people on board, and gives you a stronger picture of the right person to hire.

Here's a sample Thank-You Note for a Staff Content Designer on the Safety Team at Lyft.

> Leadership at Lyft wants to thank you for everything you've done to make Lyft safer for Riders and Drivers. In your first year you have:
>
> - Launched a new Safety hub, increasing usage of our core Safety tools by 42%
> - Evolved our Verified Rider program to include name confirmation
> - Led a session for the Safety Council on how to eliminate harassment on the platform, which led to specific initiatives for the 2026 roadmap
>
> Beyond your contributions to your product team, you've been a key member of the Content Design team as well. Thank you for:
>
> - Joining Content Design Leadership to re-evaluate our onboarding process, leading to faster onboarding for all of Design
> - Leading Content Design crit sessions, modeling collaborative crit behavior and increasing the quality of junior CDs
> - Developed a Trauma-informed Content Design standard, which scaled your knowledge and experience to the broader Design team
>
> Thank you for everything you've contributed, and we can't wait to see what you'll achieve in your next year!

The Performance Profile

After you've received your teams' feedback, it's time to put together the Performance Profile. The Performance Profile takes everything in the Thank-You Note and strategizes it. For each accomplishment detailed in the note, list out, to the point of exhaustion, every skill and strength required. Some of this might end up in the job description, some of this might be just for you and the hiring panel.

You really want to detail every single thing, warts and all. This is not your job description (we're getting there!), but it is something you might want to show your top candidate in the final round, so they can see exactly what this job is all about.

We'll grab *just one* of the bullet points from our sample Thank-You Note to see how this shakes out:

Accomplishment	How they did it
Launched a new Safety hub, increasing usage of our core Safety tools by 42%	Conduct an independent general audit into the safety space, understanding the product as it stands now and the relevant competitive landscape. Attend initial kick-offs and preliminary meetings (virtually). Set up ongoing 1:1s with key collaborators: UXR, Design, and PM Building remote relationships: UXR, Design and PM are all in SF. Work with Product Manager to define and articulate the business need, measurements of success, and milestones Conduct independent competitive audit Conduct collaborative internal audit Present audit findings to inform design direction Plan a Design Sprint with PD/UXR Lead a session of the Design Sprint Take Design Sprint outcomes and adapt into the PRD Work with UXR to define qual study approach, including what to show and recruit parameters Attend UXR sessions, taking notes and iterating materials as study progresses Participate in debriefs Inform UXR's share-out of work, and adapt into the PRD Collaborate with Science on testing plan and scale, including milestones and metrics Collaborate with Engineering to confirm tech feasibility, adjusting as needed [continues]

Accomplishment	How they did it
	Define Content Design principles for the new feature, informed by research Collaborate with Product Design to create wireframes and initial designs Co-present work at Design Crit and incorporate feedback Take work to Content Crit and incorporate feedback Prepare work for presentation to various levels of leadership, up to and including the CEO Present and articulate design decisions at said leadership presentations Develop content specs, including accessibility notes and considerations Attend tech hand-offs and walk through your work as required Monitor tickets and bugs that might have content implications Celebrate launch of M1 of the feature!

That's just one accomplishment. Rinse and repeat for the other accomplishments in the Thank-You Note.

This starts to get at some of the language of a job description. Instead of showing all the things a candidate has done, or qualifications they may have, we're beginning to paint a picture of what they will do and how they're going to do it.

Is this a long document? It is! But going through this exercise helps you truly identify the skills and strengths you must have in this candidate. What's more, it helps everyone else on your hiring team really understand this specific role that you're hiring for.

The Have/Learn Table

Now that we know what the job is going to look like and everything this person will do, we'll begin to take that into a rubric. This is how we'll determine if the candidates we're talking to are a good fit. Because we're all reasonable people, it may seem unlikely that every candidate is going to be able to do everything, right out the gate.

There's learning that happens on the job.

So we'll create a simple table for each skill or capability. If it's something they need to have from day one, it goes under "Have." If it's something they'll need to learn, you guessed it, it goes under "Learn." One thing to keep in mind: when you're putting something in the Learn" column, make sure you have the resources to teach it and/or it's a teachable skill. For example, you don't want to hire a Content Designer who is simply not a good writer (I've seen it happen you guys!).

On the other hand, say your company uses a fun and proprietary ticketing system called "UnicornTix." It was developed by an ambitious engineer during Hack Week, the CTO loves it, so everyone has learned to manage. Unless you're talking to a boomerang candidate (someone who has worked for your company, left, and is coming back), it's impossible that any candidate will come in as an expert in UnicornTix. And it would be unreasonable to expect that. So that one goes in the "Learn" column.

Continuing with our Staff Content Designer on Safety, we'll just take a look at that first entry into the Performance Profile:

"Conduct an independent audit into the safety space, understanding the product as it stands now and the relevant competitive landscape"

Have	Learn
Independent research experience Assess materials for patterns Ability to identify themes Ability to articulate themes Writing skills Ability to design presentation document Ability to speak to work Ability to answer questions and explain decisions	Facility with Google Docs Facility with Figma

This table is just for one of the skills or capabilities from just one of the accomplishments, so you could imagine how exhaustive this is going to get. But here's the thing: there's going to be a lot of repeated "haves." Many of these skills are going to come up again and again. For a Content Designer, "Writing Skills" is a core competency that will support just about each of those accomplishments.

Once you've detailed out all the Haves and the Learns, you can start to group them into categories: Technical Capabilities, Collaboration Style, Leadership. This will inform the final document.

So now we're getting a clearer view of not only the job, but the specific skills someone needs to have, right out of the gate (and the things we're willing to teach). Often you'll see these manifest in job descriptions as the 'must-haves' and 'nice-to-haves.' See? I told you we were getting closer to job description town. Just one more step!

The Assessment Criteria

Finally, we get to a hard-and-fast checklist. For each of those skills, we'll have a rubric to determine if the skills are present or not. This helps everyone from the recruiter to the hiring panel objectively assess if a given candidate has enough comparable experience to be a fit for the job.

For each skill, we'll create a scorecard. The levels are:

Basic	Adequate	Emergent	Proficient	Distinguished

Basic: they have some demonstrable ability, and can limp along

Adequate: they have proven competency, but may still require some oversight

Emergent: they can perform this skill independently, and are aware of their blind spots

Proficient: they are very good at this skill, and may begin to be teaching or coaching others

Distinguished: they are a leader in the field, may have even written a book chapter or presented at a conference about it

Now, your mileage may vary depending on the level of person you're hiring for, and what skills they have. For instance, if you're hiring for a super junior person or intern, it's ok if their skills trend more towards Basic or Adequate, providing that you have the resources in place to uplevel them during their tenure. But for our Staff Content Design position, we're going to want to see these skills land in the Emergent/Proficient space. Well enough that they can do the job while still maintaining motivation and interest, but not so far that they are going to get bored or feel like they aren't growing.

As you begin to use this tool to assess candidates, keep an eye on people who are overqualified for the role. In a tough job market, people may be applying jobs they have too much experience for, and as a hiring manager, you might think you're getting a deal. The risk there is having someone in the role get bored, phone it in, or find that they're not, in fact, satisfied doing (or earning) less.

Once you have this Assessment Criteria up and running, now you can begin to have a more robust conversation with your recruiter about writing a Job Description that isn't just a laundry list of experience, but a piece that paints a picture of the specific role, the core criteria, and will speak directly to quality candidates that are much more likely to be successful.

Takeaways

First design the job

Going straight to the job description is like going straight to code. Design the job before you start making all those bullet points.

Focus on the future of the road

Ground your thinking in what the candidate will do vs, what they have done.

Don't go it alone

Designing the job is a collaborative effort. Get insight and feedback from the people who will help hire, and ultimately work with, this person.

CHAPTER TWO

Writing job descriptions that don't suck

I really hope you didn't skip Chapter 1. It was a lot, I know. But going through the exercises listed there will not only inform the job descriptions you write, but how everyone who is on your hiring team assesses candidates from here on out. Plus, it'll make writing the actual job description a lot easier. Focusing on articulating comparable experience, relevant skills, and real accomplishments will attract the right person for the right job at the right time. Let's get to writing!

Take it from the top: Titling your Job Description

Maybe you're at one of the big FAANG (MAANG?) companies and your job titles and job ladders are already set in stone. If so, yay and I'm sorry. It seems the bigger and more established a company gets, the more inscrutable job titles become. Plus, there might be less flexibility in customizing the job description (JD) to this specific opportunity. Is "Staff" or "Principal" higher? Why does a "Senior" seem like a "Junior," but something marked "entry-level" requires five years of experience. Just how?

If you have a little more flexibility in creating a job title then, once again, yay and I'm sorry. You get to target the job title specifically to the role, but also this means a tricky Content Design problem to solve. How can you set the title in a way that sets expectations, both for level, core competency, and specific skills?

Lucky for you, I'm a Content Designer by trade and happy to help solve this problem.

Tip: the job ladder job title doesn't have to be the one you post
While the "official" title might look like **Product Designer II**, outside the context of a job ladder, it doesn't make much sense. Instead, see if you can work to post a job title that's more descriptive in terms of seniority and specifics. Maybe it's more Mid-level Product Designer, Growth or Staff Content Designer, Accessibility. Even if those aren't the Workday-official titles, they're more useful for job seekers.

Introducing: your company

For most medium-to-big size companies, the "about us" segment of the JD is already written and there's not a lot you can do about that.

And there's something to be said for consistency. It makes it easier to present the same values over and over again, and gives the benefit of a semblance of order to some of the most dysfunctional orgs. Yay them!

But maybe you have a little freedom in your job description to go beyond the required template and start to explain what your company is really all about. Maybe you can get into what your design team is about. So how do you introduce your company in a quick paragraph? Here's what to focus on:

Don't assume you're well known

Just because you're a household name in, um, your household, don't assume everyone knows anything about you. A quick summary about what your company does, the industry you're in, and what you're famous for (or want to be famous for) is a good start. And don't forget the core facts: where you're based, if you support remote/hybrid work, how many employees you have, and the company website.

Detail the team

Give a quick make-up of the design team: maybe it's different orgs (ecommerce, hardware and software), or core job types (Designers, Content Designers, Researchers and Illustrators), and maybe a little about your org structure. Is the team centralized or embedded? Reporting into something other than a VP of Design? The details and specifics matter!

Detail the culture

Do you have an annual design conference? Are you all about crits and jams? Do members of your team go out rock climbing on Mondays or have you done spontaneous whale watching trips? Consider adding in the specific culture details that set your team apart, or feel different or special to you. Make sure to mix in the things that happen during office hours (like crits and jams) as well as a diverse, inclusive array of extracurriculars (if you have them). You don't want your candidates to self-select out of applying if they're not into rock climbing or whales.

If you do get to write up a little about your company or team, do everything you can to make it as specific as possible. Anytime you end up in cliche-town, "fast-paced environment," "work hard, play hard," "disruption," you're doing less and less to stand out from the rest of the companies. Think specifically about how the company is different than other places you've worked before. Ask your colleagues, get some feedback. The intent is to show off what your values and culture are, even before your candidate starts their application.

Both the nitty and the gritty

Now, the part we've all been waiting for: the actual job description. This is where the fun begins, and this is where the specifics get even more specific. This is the part of the JD where a candidate begins to ask not just "is this the right place for me," but consider, "am I the right person for this job?" So, how do we get there?

Start with a strengths wish list

You know the job. You know what it's going to take and what the day-to-day is going to look like. This is where you put it down in black and white. Going back to the bullet points you started with, go back and stack-rank the must-haves down to the nice-to-haves. In the JD, connect the strength of what they do to how they'll put it to work.

For example, a couple of strengths might be "core writing skills," "managing your own work" and "writing collaboration." This might turn into "You project manage and write for complex initiatives, often involving other content writers, and together deliver to expected timelines and standards."

Detail a day in the life

Design at once looks a little bit the same and a little bit different at all companies. Yes, there will be heads-down time; yes, there will be meetings. But there are some key details that candidates might be looking for to see what the job is really like. That's where a day in the life comes in.

Create a list that shows what a given designer is going to be doing day in, day out. Lead with verbs (write, design, collaborate, synthesize, lead), specify with whom (other designers, project managers, engineers, marketers), to do what (build consumer-facing features, improve dashboards and internal tools, develop enterprise solutions). Drop in details about the tools, the means, and the specifics they'll be working on.

Airbnb does this in their job descriptions. This is one for a "Knowledge Strategist"

A Typical Day

- You are responsible for translating information into clear, easy to understand content across internal knowledge bases and community-facing surfaces (Help Center, Chat bots, etc.) in line with Airbnb's tone and voice standards
- Content types you maintain include FAQs, Community Support standard responses, call-scripts, short and long-form Help Center articles, how-to's and tool manuals.
- You analyze dashboard data/trends and feedback received from our front-line support staff, other users, and cross-functional partners to proactively resolve knowledge gaps
- Supported by leadership, you manage and oversee complex content and knowledge management tasks and lead initiatives that improve the accessibility and quality of our content.
- You represent CSKM in cross-functional settings with expertise on existing writing and content management practices, and an understanding of where custom solutions are needed, to navigate conversations pertaining to goals/outputs, timeline commitments and communicate risks, dependencies with leadership
- You project manage and write for complex initiatives, often involving other content writers, and together deliver to expected timelines and standards.
- You influence Airbnb's tone/voice standards, and shape CSKM tone/voice standards with Airbnb's standards in mind
- You mentor other members of the team in your areas of expertise and optimizing the team's ways of working
- You partner with colleagues from other teams such as to deliver creative knowledge solutions that enhance the user and/or ambassador experiences

I like that it leads with "you," so it's allowing the candidate to picture themselves in the role, doing these tasks, and positions them to see if they can visualize doing these tasks, having this job.

On the other hand, you could keep these a lot shorter by leading with verbs and just cutting to the chase. The style choice is yours!

Ultimately, when you're writing the job description, the core details themselves, you want to strike a fine balance between the must-haves and the nice to haves. Lead with the things you for sure need to have in this candidate: specific domain knowledge, tools expertise, strength in a particular design skill. From there, it should evolve more and more into a wish list.

A note from HR

Job descriptions are a place where bias comes to play: ageism, experience bias, native-language requirements. They're everywhere. Here are a few (sadly) common mistakes and how to avoid them:

Focusing too much on career state
"Recent grad" "entry-level" "mid-level" "mature." These terms are speaking much more to someone's age than to their experience, expertise, and special skills. You might have someone who graduated a long time ago, but is taking a turn in their career. You might have a mother returning to the workforce. You might have a great candidate who spent time in the military. There's a ton of reasons why a candidate might have a gap, delay, or pause in their resume. Most of them are not a concern to you. Position the role in terms of skills and strengths, and less about where they are in their career.

Requirements that exclude
"Native speaker" "higher education graduate" "four-year university." You might have a certain candidate in mind, or have ideas about what comes along with these labels or checkboxes. But putting these in

your job description means excluding a wide swath of people. Instead of looking for a "native speaker," you might speak to fluency requirements. Instead of degree or institution requirements, consider the skills you associate with someone who's a college grad. Reasoning? Analytics? Research? Sure, I've got a degree in Russian Language and Literature, but does that have anything to do with my competency as a Content Designer? Not really!

"Culture fit" or, worse "culture add"

What a term, right? It could mean just about anything: race, personality, neurodiversity, gender. Even hobbies. It's a broad term that might aim to be inclusive, but can easily have the opposite effect. Company culture is a real thing, don't get me wrong. But instead of adding an opaque term like "culture fit," dig deep into the aspects of your company culture that matter, and put those in the job description.

That might look like:

- How you make decisions
- How the teams are structured
- What team-building activities look like
- What perks and benefits you offer

And keep an eye on other coded language, that might also be exclusive: "work hard, play hard". "Company happy hours," anything referring to the company as a "family." Some people at your company may absolutely want their whole lives to be about their job, including hanging out with colleagues after the last meeting of the day or heading to the bar to celebrate a launch. And that's great, but it shouldn't be a requirement for doing a competent job, meeting company goals, or getting the work done.

Takeaways

Job descriptions should paint a picture of your ideal candidate (but not be too narrow)
Be specific about the skills and strengths required and the kind of work they'll be doing. Lead with the must-haves and leave room for interpretation.

Be wary of bias and non-inclusive language
Double-check for terms that might turn people off. Keep an eye out for ageism, sexism, or particular language requirements.

Use a "day-in-the-life" styling to highlight the strengths you want to see in candidates
Scannable bullet points can get to the heart of what the job is really about. Lead with verbs and be specific.

CHAPTER THREE

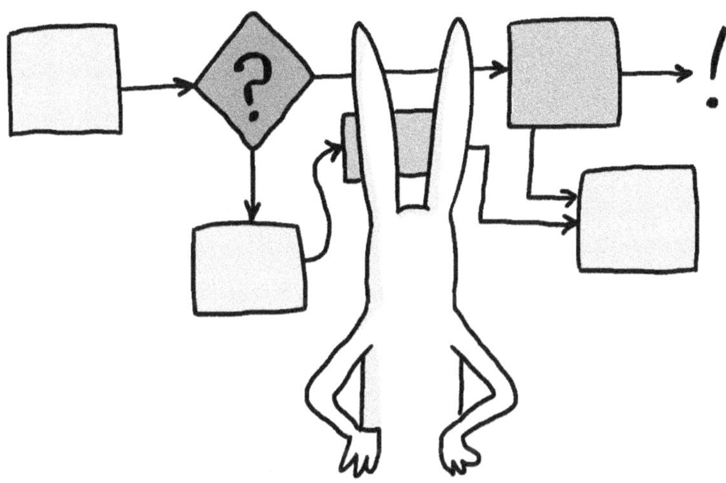

Designing your interview process

So, your job description is all done and you're ready to get it posted on the company site, promote it on LinkedIn, and tell all your friends and colleagues about this incredible person you're going to hire, right? Wait! What are you going to do when you start to get actual human candidates applying for the job? How are you going to know who's right, who's not quite right, and then the whole group of people you're not sure about, but your gut tells you maybe?

That's where designing an interview process comes in.

Interview processes are not one-size-fits-all. To be fair, consistent and equitable, you want to make sure you're putting all the candidates through the same process for the same job. That said, you can absolutely adapt your process to the job you've posted. You might omit or add steps based on:

- Contract or full-time role
- If this position exists already or if it's new to the company
- Urgency of the hire
- Engagement (long-term vs short-term hire)
- Seniority of the role

In this chapter we'll talk about the types of interviews you might include in your process, how to choose which ones to include, plus everyone's favorite topic: the design exercise.

Types of interviews

You remember this, don't you? It couldn't have been that long ago you were out there, looking for a job. Submitting resumes, hoping for an email back. And then that feeling: a heady mix of dread and anticipation, worry and excitement. Then the interviews begin, and then that feeling continues as you move through the process: from screening to hiring manager, to cross-functional interviews, to maybe panels and more. It can be a lot. So let's dig into the kinds of different interviews, the functions they serve, and how to decide if you want them in your interview process.

Recruiter screens

Once you've approved a few resumes, recruiters will set up a screening call for those candidates. Typically, these are relatively quick, 30-minute calls to get a top-level assessment of the candidate: does what they say seem to match up with their resume, maybe a little bit about why they're looking for a job or why they're interested in this particular role, doing a little digging on some of those specifics you asked about, plus getting into some of the logistics (remote vs in-person, salary expectations.) They'll also ask a candidate about any accessibility needs or accommodations they might have. If they make it through that gauntlet, they'll be passed along to you for a hiring manager screen.

Hiring manager screens

Finally, you get to meet some candidates! Hiring manager screens are your first opportunity to get to know a candidate, better understand their skillsets and background, and generally get a feel for what they're about. This is also a key point in deciding if they should move forward or not.

Panel interviews

Next up is a panel interview. This might look like a Designer presenting some case studies, walking through a design exercise (if you assigned one). The people present at the panel interview can vary depending on your goals and how this person is going to fit in the organization. You can have a single-discipline panel (all Designers, all Content Designers, all Researchers), or mix it up with a mixed design or entirely cross-functional panel.

1:1 interviews

Just like it says on the label, 1:1 interviews allow the candidate to have one-on-one chats with people in your org. Usually, this includes people who were present at the panel interview, so they can follow up on any questions they had during that presentation or discussion. You'll be in charge of writing an interview guide to help the interviewers structure the conversation. You might direct the 1:1s to go after a specific angle (collaboration! Core skills!), or you can give your interviewers a little more free rein.

Final chats

At the end of an interview process, it's often nice to have one more check-in with a candidate, especially if you're feeling really promising about them. Giving them an extra 30 minutes of your time to allow them to ask any questions, or for you to follow up on any outlying areas can be time excessively well spent. It's kinda like parking meter math: an extra quarter can save you from getting a $97 ticket. And an extra 30 minutes of your time can save you from making a suboptimal hire.

Hot takes: the design exercise

> "I know people don't like them, but I'm still a fan. The more lightweight, the better. Especially in the writing roles, it's crucial to get a fair assessment of their core skills and competencies."
> -Frank Marquardt, Head of Content Design at Yahoo

Ask the LinkedIn community what their opinions are about design exercises, and you'll find yourself wishing you had actually gone into a forest to find a literal bear to poke. The takes, they are hot. The opinions, they are strong. The prevailing opinion from candidates does seem to be: they are awful, please don't. On the other hand, they can still be a really useful benchmark for hiring managers.

- **They don't generally reflect how actual work is done.** The Designer doesn't really have sufficient context to make informed recommendations, plus they may be uninformed in specific product language that might result in distracting errors.

- **They take up (unpaid) time.** Interviewing is time-consuming enough as it is. Adding in an assignment might mean another

1-10 hours, depending on how much time the candidate decides to put in (even if you put in the instructions to limit how much time is spent). And one candidate may not have as much time as another to do the assignment. It's not an even assessment.

- **They run the risk of being perceived as free work.** I have never heard of people actually taking design candidates' work and implementing it, but it seems reasonable that if you're reviewing real product that real suggestions might end up live – because they are clear and obvious improvements that someone already suggested.

When I was in ad school, we were given an assignment to come up with a simple ad for Dramamine, where it was just a product shot and a headline under five words. I thought I had nailed it, and I was a brilliant copywriting genius. "Travel insurance." I was so, so confident walking into class and taping up my comp. Until I looked around and saw about three-quarters of the class had come up with the exact same idea.

So it would make sense that if someone is given a design exercise that reflects soon-to-be-shipped product, and they make a very obvious suggestion, and then see it live, that they think they've given a company free work.

So if you're considering a design exercise as part of your interview process, maybe consider these points:

What are you looking to learn, and can you do that in the interview process itself?
If you're looking to see UX approaches, design thinking, or how a candidate might take on an ambiguous problem, can you do it live? Look through some fake mocks or a competitive product together.

Ask the candidate to articulate what they might change, what questions they would ask, or what context they might need to get started.

Can you pay people for their time?

If you're intent on doing a take-home exercise, can you find budget to pay people for their time? It removes the perception of free work, plus it shows from the gate that you value the candidate and their time spent.

Right-sizing your process

Not all jobs are created equal and not all job processes should be exactly the same. Does a short-term contract need a full portfolio review and panel presentation? Probably not! Would you hire a high-level Design VP with just a recruiter screen? Seems unlikely! So how do you know what to leave in, and what to leave out?

Work with your recruiter to determine what you'd like to do, but in the broadest sense, you can take a scaled approach: the simpler/smaller the job, the more truncated the process can be. Big job? Don't skip a step.

Designing an interview process will really depend on the role you're hiring in the context of the organization you're hiring into. Essentially: the bigger the process, the more opinions you're seeking to find consensus. And there are all kinds of reasons you might be building that consensus:

A tricky political situation

Maybe you're working in a consensus-driven environment, and you need everyone on board before any move is made. Seems tough, but also familiar. Even though you're the hiring manager, maybe you don't have the trust of everyone in the organization yet, and you need to get their buy-in to make sure the candidate is set up for success (ew, that was a really corporate sentence).

Hiring for a very specific skillset that you don't understand

Hey, it's ok if you don't know everything about your particular job function. Do I understand the concept of "taxonomy" more than my mother? Yes. Would I hire me as a Taxonomist? No, sir, I would not. When hiring for a specific skillset that's a little outside your realm, it's good to gather a slightly broader group of opinions to confirm the hire is right.

Hiring for someone else

In a past job, I was often tasked with hiring Content Design contractors that I, myself, wasn't going to manage. Their day-to-day would be overseen by a Design manager, and I wouldn't be too involved in their work. While my general approach to hiring contractors was to keep the process limited, I would extend it to include their future manager as well as a peer or two. The right fit is more than *just* about skills, but about collaboration and chemistry too. I wanted to make sure that it was a good fit, and not just (boop!) plopping a new contractor on their doorstep for them to adopt and love forever.

Working with recruiters

From big, massive companies to little start-ups, you're likely to be working with a recruiter. Also, the term "recruiter" is a pretty crappy one. While they certainly can be out there, soliciting and finding candidates, these days they're more on the front line of the deluge of candidates that are coming in. They help sort who should move forward, who should be (gently, kindly) passed on, and are your very best friend in designing this interview process. And if you're working at one of those massive companies, this entire process might be set for you, but it's still good to know what to expect in general.

There are two kinds of recruiters you're likely to come across: internal and external.

Internal recruiters are on staff at your company, are likely very well-versed in company culture and roles, and are very familiar with the product. Big companies might even have very specialized recruiters for individual disciplines. When I was at Facebook, we had at least three recruiters just for Content Design alone!

External recruiters are usually found at staffing agencies. They are most often used to help quickly fill short-term or contract roles. External recruiters may have less familiarity with the discipline you're hiring for, with the specifics of the role, and with company culture. External recruiters and their companies will handle the contract of the person hired, and will charge a mark-up to your company. Note: sometimes external recruiters can be a little bit more urgent and, well, pushy than your internal recruiter. This is because they are usually motivated by getting the role filled as quickly as possible, so the company can start earning on your hire (a reasonable motivation!). Be firm in your expectations, be confident in your timeline, and don't feel pressured to hire a candidate because they want to get it done!

With both internal and external recruiters, it's important to have an initial kick-off call for the role, so you can discuss what you're looking for in terms of key experience, strengths, plus any 'nice-to-haves', as well as the specific logistics around interviewing. Recruiters will be fielding resumes, so you'll want to give them a list of the things you'd like to see in a candidate.

This might look like:

- Specific domain experience (Finance? Health? Hardware? AI?)
- Tools (Figma? Google suite? Microsoft? Writer?)
- Years of experience
- Leadership and experience managing direct reports
- Skillsets (audits, content management, design systems, public speaking)

Once your kick-off call is done, then your job should get posted and you're off to the races. Recruiters will send you batches of resumes to review, and you'll be able to decide who you'd like to chat with, and who you'd like to pass on. In general, recruiters love feedback. If they keep sending you resumes that aren't what you're looking for, let them know what you see that they didn't. For both internal and external recruiters, make sure you're touching base and having regular calls to make sure you're really clear on what you're looking for.

Oh, and be kind and responsive to your recruiters, no matter if they are internal or external. They are an expert in your corner to help you along in the process. Help them help you, and be timely in your response.

When talking to Christina (Maz) Mazurowski, Product Recruiter at Datadog, she said,

"The hardest thing is when hiring managers don't get in feedback right away, As a candidate, the very least a company can do is give you a yes/no within 48 hours. And at least be communicative with a timing expectation. A lot of the time recruiters can't give an outcome in a timely manner is because they're chasing hiring managers."

Takeaways

Right-size your interview plan

Not every job requires the same interview structure. Design one that matches the role you're seeking to fill.

Rethink design exercises

Is there another way you can assess skill and design chops? A live exercise or talking through a portfolio might be more fair to all candidates.

Befriend your recruiter

Work with them closely to help craft your job description and confirm you have the same candidate profile in mind.

CHAPTER FOUR

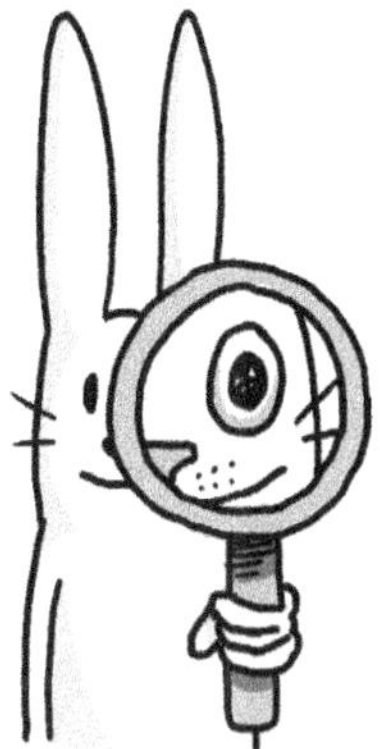

Reading resumes and decoding portfolios

How exciting! The job is posted, applicants have been coming in, and now your recruiter (or your online robot hiring assistant) has some resumes for you to review. You've been waiting for this, you have all the strengths in mind that you're looking for, and you can picture the perfect candidate already. You can see them in meetings, raising their hand, coming in with unbelievable insights, shipping beautiful work, and the whole team gets together to throw a party, just for you, just for hiring them.

<record scratch> Sorry! Throw all that away! Clear your mind of any image of the candidate, any expectation. In reviewing resumes and portfolios, the first thing you want to do is open your mind, while

at the same time, interrogating yourself for bias. You at once need to read between the lines, while considering every little detail. You need to go with your instinct, but also question what that instinct has been informed by. It's a lot!

But there's a way: we'll talk about how to start by checking your bias again and again, how to read resumes for their story, and how to decode portfolios to see what they're really trying to say.

Check yourself, else you wreck yourself

If you've been through any kind of corporate training in the past decade, you've probably clicked through an online program or sat through a training about unconscious bias. I hope you were paying attention, but just in case you weren't, unconscious biases inform how we make decisions. They're informed by our experiences, both social and personal.

David Dylan Thomas, author of the must-read *Design for Cognitive Bias*, explains that they're a series of shortcuts that are sometimes innocuous, but often super dangerous. "When I learned that something as evil as racial or sexual bias could be boiled down to something as simple as pattern recognition, I decided I needed to learn everything I could about cognitive bias."

While those fancy trainings were probably focused on in-person acts of bias, you better believe there are all kinds of biases that can pop up when you're reading resumes. The act of reviewing resumes challenges you to make a snap judgment based on little information: that's where bias thrives!

You might be aware of gender and racial bias, but consider if you have preconceived ideas about what makes a good education, what companies are impressive to you, or experience that you might consider a red flag. Biases can work both ways: you might give more credence to a candidate you think has impressive experience because they worked at OMG Mega Corp, or you might end up dismissing a candidate because they've only worked in failed start-ups.

The best way to combat bias is to get acquainted with it, so let's get to work:

Race and gender bias: who they are

We have a homogeny problem in design. Go to a design conference, and you'll see a lot of the same types of people: mainly white, mainly women in Content Design, men in product design. This is a gross overstatement, but the perception is there. Are there a lot of people of color and gender across all of UX? Absolutely. Let's make it even more.

Race and gender show up primarily in names and education spaces in resumes. You might see a foreign-sounding name and make a snap judgment and stop reading the rest of their resume. You might see a university in a country other than the one you're in and think "does Latvia even do UX?" And that's a weird question.

Company bias: where they've worked

Once upon a time, having a FAANG (MAANG?) company on a resume was all anyone needed to see. The company would become attached to the candidates name, a tacit endorsement. "Former Google designer," "just left a UXR position at Netflix." Now? It can actually go the other way: people who have been at one of those biggies for a long time might be perceived as too spoiled, too entrenched in one way of working, or just too out of touch. It's messed up, right?

Beyond just the big companies, you might see particular experience that doesn't align with your personal values or beliefs: like someone who lists work with religious institutions, a non-profit, or other cause. For instance, how would you feel about a candidate that had done work with the NRA? What about Planned Parenthood? If you are committed to finding the right candidate with the right strengths, you have to look beyond your own bias. It's really hard.

Experience bias: how long they've worked

Let's say you are 100% sure you need a super senior IC who can hit the ground running independently on a very particular superset of product communication in the financial sector. They must have at least five years of experience in this very thing, plus a foundation of other experience beforehand. You'll settle for nothing less. But then you see a resume come through of a more mid-level person, and their last three years was at a big financial institution, working on comms.

Seems like maybe someone to talk to, right? Right. Erase from your mind how much experience you think a person needs to have had in a particular field or place. Instead, consider how much comparable experience they have, regardless of tenure. Also, keep an eye out for those strengths: do you see a match between what they've worked on and what you're looking for? Maybe worth a conversation.

Age bias

Too young to have enough experience? Too old to still be curious and be tech-savvy? Stop it right this minute. I see you, seeing how long someone's been working, checking when they graduated college, doing some math. Again, I challenge you to look for someone's strengths, consider their relevant experience, and open your mind to talking to someone a little older or a little younger than you thought you might consider.

Discrimination based on age, beyond being illegal, may also rob you of a really great candidate. Nathan, a colleague at Lyft, got a late start in his UX career, because he took a detour through journalism, art, and a time experiencing homelessness. He found his way out, and by someone taking a chance on him, he's become one of the most competent, eager-to-learn and empathetic Content Designers I've worked with. We're the same age: he's pretty junior and I'm not. He has an entire career ahead of him, and it has a lot to do with someone not dismissing his resume when it looked like he had a bit of a non-conventional career path.

Age is just a number. Don't listen to Indeed.

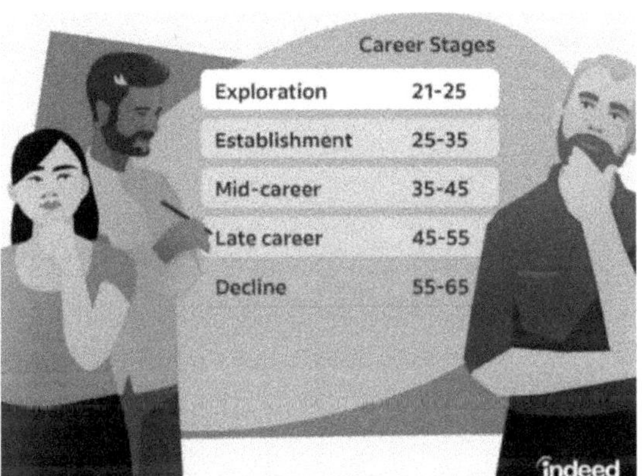

Ok, now that you have solved all your bias problems, you're ready to go! Kidding! Checking your bias is something you just have to work on, forever and ever. Be aware, give yourself a little more time to review resumes, and continue to keep tabs on your own instincts.

Reading resumes for story

Every resume has a story in it: where someone's from, the twists and turns their education or career took. Each step should reveal a little more about them: why they chose that job, what they're drawn to, the kinds of things they want to do next. It's up to you to find that story, find those self-reported strengths, and see if they align with what you're looking for.

When I advise job seekers how to write their resume, I tell them that they're constructing a narrative, and that the next chapter in that story is the job their applying for. What you need to review as a hiring manager is: could the next step of this person's journey be this job?

Things you might ask as you read a resume:

- What is the throughline of their career so far?
- What has been a consistent interest or area of focus?
- Where have they developed or grown?
- What have they highlighted in terms of accomplishments?

These themes will point you to their strengths, what they love doing, what's important and rewarding for them. This might look like particular expertise, domain knowledge, skills or tools. All the things you need to know to see if you want to have a conversation with them.

Reading resumes for strengths

Hot take: when reading resumes, ignore job titles, places of work, education. Instead read for strengths and interests.

When you set up this job, you had a list of strengths and areas of interest this person would have, remember? Now it's time to go back to that list, and keep it in mind as you read through resumes. Assess for the skills, for the domain expertise. Try and understand how this person thrives, what gets them engaged and interested, what they're most proud of. How does that align with what you're looking for?

Reading resumes for strengths is a great way to solve for bias and see the story behind the structure of a resume.

And if you're deciding whether or not to move forward with a person, maybe listen to your curiosity. If something catches your eye, or if you're not sure, maybe consider having that screening call with them. You might just be surprised who you end up chatting with.

Scanning portfolios

If you've taken the next step past resumes and into a little portfolio review, take the same approach: you're looking to find a match between what you need and what this person is all about. Now, you'll likely be digging into someone's case studies a little deeper further down in the interview process, but here are some things to keep in mind in that first portfolio review:

Pobudy's Nerfect

Man, I used to be a real super jerk about typos and formatting issues. And sometimes I still am, but I'm a little more gracious than I used to be. It comes down to context: if you're hiring a proofreader or a solo content person who is going to be 100% responsible for perfect content, then I think it's ok to be strict. If you're hiring a Designer, or a content person who is going to be part of a team, or just about any other job, I think it's ok to forgive a mistake or two, especially if there's a lot more to a candidate that you're compelled by.

I was once applying to a Very Big Job, and I wanted to be as quick as I could in my replies to them. They asked me for some work samples, and because this Very Big Job was at a very design-centric company, I didn't want to rely on my old portfolio. Working quickly, and in an effort to impress them, I redesigned one of my case studies. "Move fast!" I thought. Well, in moving too quickly and editing too ruthlessly, I let a couple of repeated words slip in. I sent it along without realizing. Thankfully, the recruiter caught them and gave me a heads up.

I was *mortified* and incredibly thankful for their grace.

I wrote, "I just wanted to drop you a note and thank you again for giving me the opportunity to correct my mistakes. You absolutely didn't have to do that, and I sincerely appreciate you looking out for me.

"I had such great conversations with you and [the hiring manager], and I imagine my enthusiasm about the role propelled me a little too quickly to get my work to you. I don't generally ascribe to 'move fast and break things' for this very reason!"

Looking beyond products, deliverables and impact
Just as you don't want to be swayed by your bias about a certain company or experience, don't let bias about a certain product or feature get in your way when reviewing a portfolio. Maybe you have zero interest in video games, but you're reviewing the work of someone who's been in gaming for years. How can you look past a domain that you don't understand, and instead consider the story the candidate is telling: what did they do, what are they proud of, what did they overcome, and what drives them?

Don't get hung up on metrics and numbers either. We've all been on those projects that, despite everyone's best effort, either fail to launch or just simply fail. I worked on an entire app at Google for a year, just to have the plug pulled a few days before launch. That was a fun day. But even though I didn't have great numbers or a killer product story to show from it, in that year I learned how to be a Content Designer, how to collaborate with Design, how to build a messaging matrix from scratch, and how to establish a new discipline when I was learning what it all meant myself. Even though I didn't walk away with beautiful metrics, I did walk away with exponentially more experience than I started that job with.

Reading for the narrative: problem, constraints, obstacles, solutions

Just as we read resumes for a story, we should do the same when reading case studies. Beyond tearing apart the details of the design or content choices, keep yourself grounded in trying to read the broader narrative. What was the problem they were trying to solve? What constraints were they working under? What obstacles did they overcome? What solutions did they come up with and what was the overall impact? These questions, not the radius of their button corners, will give insight into what kind of Designer they are, what kind of person they are to work with, and most importantly, what's crucial and interesting to them as a Designer.

Takeaways

Check your bias. Then check it again.

When you're quick to dismiss, give it a second thought. Be self-aware, and go slow.

Read resumes for news you can use

Review resumes by looking for a match to the skills and strengths this job requires. Keep an open mind, and consider how relevant experience could be applicable to the tasks at hand.

Consider portfolios carefully

Dig deep into intention, framing, and the work behind the work. What does a given case study show about what this candidate is interested in, or how they thrive.

CHAPTER FIVE

Getting the best out of an interview

While many steps in the interview process are important, I'd argue that the hiring manager interview is the most crucial one. The job description got the candidate in the door, they looked good enough on paper to get through it, and they passed a recruiter screen. So they're not a psychopath (maybe). But this is your 30-minute shot to see if they should spend their time getting a presentation together and if you want to spend some of your teams' precious time interviewing.

All you have to do is have a 30-minute conversation to interrogate their background (while keeping them comfortable), give them enough context about the company, the role, and yourself (without eating up all their time), and still leave plenty of time for questions at the end. No pressure!

It can be done. I've done it. Hundreds of times. And each time, while I do have a set structure, I'm able to conduct an insightful, efficient conversation that doesn't answer all my questions, but instead answers this crucial one: "Do I want to see more?"

> "It's the hiring manager's job to be a close listener to what the person is saying. To listen for what skills they've developed, what their path has been, and most importantly, does their path show development in the skills that are important for this role?"
> -Frank Maquardt, Head of Content Design, Yahoo

It's an interview, sure. But it's also a little like a first date. You're not going down the aisle after one drink, but maybe you'll meet them for dinner again sometime.

A touch of meeting etiquette

The term "etiquette" gets a bad rap. Sounds fussy and old-fashioned, but it's useful here. The point is that there are some practices in place that are worth following. Like a first date, you really want to be on your best behavior for a hiring manager interview. This means being focused, present, and respecting the candidate's time. Simple things make a big difference.

Go do not disturb and don't multi-task

In the middle of a workday, notifications are just waiting to steal your attention and compel you to tend to one fire or another. They can wait. Quit apps that generate notifications, use "do not disturb" to silence notifications, and keep your focus on this one task for the 30 minutes. Assuming you're doing a video interview, it's obvious when someone's attention is drifting all over the screen. Nod, listen, and be present.

Minimize distractions

Beyond the notifications in front of you, consider what the candidate is seeing behind you (again, assuming Zoom). If you're working from home, maybe blur out your background if you want to stay a bit more anonymous and focused on the candidate. I have a really cool Talking Heads poster behind me in my home office/dining room, and it tends to draw attention away. And if you end up with a cat-on-the-keyboard scenario like I often do, consider closing the door, just for the duration.

Know your note-taking style

Despite functionally being a writer for a living, I have the worst handwriting in the world. It's slow, it's messy, and it's useless to me when I need to refer to anything I've written down. Typing though? Savant-level. I can type notes in real-time without looking, without breaking eye contact. So when I'm interviewing, it's important to me that I'm able to type to take notes. I always tell candidates, 'I'm going to be typing while we're talking, so I can remember what we talked about. Believe me, it's better for you and for me!'

Set up your note structure beforehand

Less etiquette, just more good prep. I like to have a new doc for each candidate, and I'll set up a "pros" section, a "concerns" section, then an area for free-form notes. This is also where my scorecard comes in that I created at the outset of the job. A reminder:

For each skill, we'll create a scorecard. The levels are:

Basic	Adequate	Emergent	Proficient	Distinguished

Basic: they have some demonstrable ability, and can limp along

Adequate: they have proven competency, but may still require some oversight

Emergent: they can perform this skill independently, and are aware of their blind spots

Proficient: they are very good at this skill, and may begin to be teaching or coaching others

Distinguished: they are a leader in the field, may have even written a book chapter or presented at a conference about it

Wait until the interview is over to fill out the scorecard, but keep the skills you're assessing fresh in your mind before you start.

Schedule strategically

When we're at work, we're context-switching all the time. Running from meeting to meeting, from project to project. Getting an interview in the middle of all that can be the most difficult, and the most high-risk. These 30 minutes are crucial, so make sure you have enough time to do it right. This looks like buffering a little bit of time before and after. Before you show up, find time to orient yourself, find focus, minimize distractions and prepare. Leave a little time after the scheduled interview just in case things run over and so you have enough time to work on your notes and scorecard.

Ok, now let's get to the interview!

A structured conversation

The best interviews feel like natural conversations: you're digging into a cool area of interest, both people are participating equally. You hang up the call not just having checked the "I did the interview" box, but hopefully having learned something. This doesn't just happen.

An interview takes design, takes planning, and takes a bit of structure. Without structure, it doesn't really work for anyone.

> "I found a really cool start-up, that had a cool product. I had a couple of screening interviews first, had done quite a bit of research, and then I was going to talk to one of the founders on the phone. He hopped on and was like 'Alright, what's up?' and I was like 'Uh, hi, how do you want to do this?' And he's like 'I don't know, tell me your story,' and his whole tone was so arrogant. I was like 'I don't know how to take this,' and he was like 'if you're going to work here, people think on their feet.' The call lasted about 10 minutes, and I never heard from them again."
> -Rob Surrency, Product Designer

Now, a question like "Tell me your story," can absolutely work as a warm-up, get-to-know-you interview question. And something that open-ended can give you some useful insight into a candidate's skills in terms of working in ambiguity, storytelling, and structuring information. But without setting a roadmap and some core expectations of how the conversation is going to go, the whole thing can feel unmoored from the start.

Here's a useful outline I use for my hiring manager interviews:

- Get settled, sorted, and set expectations about the conversation (5 mins)
- Share context about you, the role, the org structure (5 mins)

- Ask them 3-4 core questions (12-15 mins, depending on their answers)
- Hiring manager "Ask me Anything" (5 mins)

We'll dig into each one and how they work.

Get ready: intros and getting settled

If you're going to have a good, relaxed conversation, you need to set the space a little bit. Even the most tenured candidates get super nervous at interviews, and it's your job to make them feel at ease. Here are a few points to hit in your first five minutes:

Introduce yourself

"Hi, I'm Robert Carpenter and I lead the Research team at Ducks, Inc."

Yep. Don't forget this bit. If you're going to have a conversation, you should know who you're having it with. Offer your name and your title, or job function.

Do a touch-base

"Thanks for taking time to chat with me today. Is now still a good time to talk?"

Right off the bat, show that you're respectful of their time, and you're setting this up as a chat, not an interrogation. Also, make sure they're ok. And as we all know, life happens between meetings. Maybe they just got a piece of bad news, or maybe their partner is about to grind some coffee and introduce an imminent interruption. Give them the chance to engage the conversation and proceed.

Set the roadmap

"I'm going to tell you a bit about the role, then I'm going to ask you a few questions. I'll make sure to leave some time at the end for you to ask me anything you want."

In order to keep building a base of comfort and respect, let them know what the next 30 minutes will look like. This is usually where I tell them that I'll be taking notes on my computer (vs. in a notebook).

The bit "anything you want" is intentionally open and vague. I really want the candidate to feel comfortable and welcome. Also, it gives them some time during my intro spiel to write questions down.

All that should take less than five minutes. Just enough to make sure everyone's opted in, comfortable, and ready to hit the proverbial road.

A tight 5 of context

While there might be a lot out there on the internet about your company or the role, or even yourself, for your candidate to research (if they did, we hope they did!), there's still something about hearing the narrative from the hiring manager. Besides, they're there to get to know you just as you're there to get to know them. A little 5-minute spiel on your journey, your role, or any other relevant context gives them some useful information.

Also, sneakily, I find that I'm asked the same questions in interviews at the end. I like to use this time to get ahead of those basics. This usually leads to a more individualized and interesting conversation throughout.

About you

While this interview isn't totally about you, it's also a little bit about you. I generally like to explain how long I've been at the role, and a little high-level view of the path that led me here. Yes, they may have read my LinkedIn, but it's possible they didn't! Besides, you can fill in some of the gaps that don't show up on the internet, like reporting structure or recent promotions.

"So I've been at Ducks, Inc. for about two years. Before that I worked at big places like Google, Twitter and Facebook. I also did a short stint at a start-up to see if it was for me. Turns out it wasn't! Right now I lead the entire Research team, and I report to the VP of Design."

A little lore

Depending on the job, the company or the market climate, there's a few different pieces of context that might be useful next. Some people might want to hear about how the company got started, others might want to dig deeper into org structure. For most Content Designers, understanding how Content Design was started and grew can be illuminating about what it's like to work at any given company.

"Research started on the ecommerce side of the house. The Design lead saw a need for people who could research, and started out with two freelancers. That need quickly grew up to a team of four full-time staff. Then I came in to grow and support the discipline. About a year and a half ago, we had a good re-org that brought two design teams together: ecommerce and Product. Product had never had Research. Sad, I know. So then I was able to seed the discipline there, and grow it. So now there's a total of eight Research staff, me included. This role will make it 9!"

Facts!

This is the place to get ahead of some basic questions that they might be asking you later. The idea here isn't to throw them off their game (mean, sneaky, not the point), but to get to more interesting conversation topics that are a level deeper than superficial job stuff. This might include:

- Company location and working hours (especially if complicated by remote work)
- Most common tools they'll encounter
- What cross-functional roles they'll be working with
- Ratios within the design team (Content Design; Product Design, or to Research, or to PM)
- <your fun facts here>

Boom. Done. In under 10 minutes, you have done so much. You've made your candidate feel comfortable. You've set expectations and offered relevant context. You've let them get to know you and the role a little bit. You've probably answered some of their questions.

Now it's time for them to start talking!

The same questions I always ask

Writing your always-ask interview questions is a fun, but challenging, exercise in content design. You need to deliver a few, scalable outputs that take into consideration:

- The goal(s) of your content
- How the candidate might feel vs. how you want them to feel

When writing your questions, think about any assumptions you'd want to clarify, particular experience you'd like to determine, or anything else that facilitates an open and honest conversation about the candidate and their background and abilities.

In my experience, people define Content Design (or content strategy, or UX writing) in all kinds of ways. One of my goals is to make sure that we're both talking about the same kind of Content Design practice: one that collaborates closely with design and research to create informed, useful user experiences in products.

Also, as a hiring manager, I want to make sure that the strengths of a given candidate are aligned with the role I'm trying to fill.

Here are my core questions, and how they serve my content constraints:

Question #1: "Everyone's path to Content Design is a little different. Tell me about how you got to where you are."

Question goal:	Confirm we're talking about the same rough definition of Content Design
Candidates feelings:	Since this is the first question, they might be feeling anxious. I want to make them feel relaxed, quickly.

Why this works: Letting people tell their own story, in their own words, immediately puts them at ease. They're used to doing it. By giving them permission to tell their story, and framing it that there's no singular "right" answer, they feel more comfortable to talk about themselves. From my point of view, I get to hear their definition of Content Design by what they've done and the path their career took.

Question #2 "What are the Content Design tasks you love to do: the ones where time goes away and you think 'yes, this is exactly why I'm in this field.'"

Question goal:	Determine the candidate's strengths, to confirm they align with the role
Candidates feelings:	This question is intended to make them feel confident, without worrying they are being arrogant.

Why this works: My approach to management and allocation is all about strengths. Tell me what you're amazing at, and I want to make sure you're spending all of your time doing that thing. This question gets people talking and excited about what their favorite aspect of their job is, and it tells me if there's a match between what they love to do, and the role I'm seeking to fill.

Question #3 "What are the Content Design tasks you might put off, or maybe feel relieved when someone takes them off your plate?"

Question goal:	Determine the candidates self-professed areas of improvement, and also telegraph that they can be open and honest with me.
Candidates feelings:	At this point they should feel comfortable, so wanting to open the door even further.

Why this works: With the first two questions, I've intentionally made the candidate feel comfortable, and that I'm simply getting to know them (which is true). This last question, which would be too scary to put first, allows me to really assess if their skillset is the right match for the job. If someone says, "to be honest, I don't love content audits," and I'm hiring for a role that has a lot of content audits, I may decline to move forward.

Wrapping it up

Flip the script: candidate questions

By this point, you should have about 5-7 minutes left in the conversation. This should leave enough time for them to ask you questions and send them on their way. Now at the beginning of the conversation, when we were setting up the roadmap, the phrase I used was "you'll have time at the end to ask me anything you want." The intent here was to set the candidate at ease and let them know that you're as open and honest as you'd want them to be!

Also, in your intro, you hopefully got ahead of some of the fact-based questions that people often ask (what are the working hours, what's the Designer : Content Designer ratio like). This means the candidate might get to some more interesting questions for you to answer.

Write down whatever questions they ask you in your notes, so you can refer to them later.

Answer any question openly and honestly. Remember, candidates should be interviewing you as well, making sure it's as good a fit for them, as it is for you.

Conclude in style

I've been doing these interviews for over a decade, and for the longest time I still stumbled on how to end the call without saying "Yeah no bye forever" and "Omg I want to hire you right now." On one hand, you want to leave them feeling reassured and heard, on the other hand, you don't want to set up a ton of false hope (or worse, lead them on).

To close, I simply like to show some appreciation, while avoiding making any promises about the next steps.

"Thanks so much for your time today. We'll be in touch soon! Enjoy the rest of your day."

Simple, right? Keep it in mind. You don't want to end up saying "We'll schedule your panel soon" or "the recruiter will follow up," since those might either be too promising or too defeating. Keep it light, keep it non-committal. When you get it wrong, it can set hopes way too high for a candidate.

> "I was looking for a different opportunity, and a Lead Product Designer position came around at an outdoors company. And I knew someone there. I applied, and the conversation with the recruiter went well. After that I spent hours preparing a presentation for the upcoming hiring manager interview. It took about 30 hours over the course of several days. The chat with the hiring manager went well! Not only was the work landing, but he gave me coaching on what I needed to change in advance of talking with the founder later that week. It never got scheduled, and my emails went unanswered. Finally I heard back from them: they weren't moving me forward, that I didn't have the experience they were looking for. They wanted more scale, more impact. During the time of this interview, I had gotten so invested, not just my time, but emotionally. The hiring manager really set me up like I was moving forward, and he never really intended to. I still haven't recovered."
> -Rob Surrency, Product Designer

Making a call: assessing if you should move the candidate through or not

After your interview is over, do everything you can to write your notes right away (even if you don't submit them until later). While the conversation is fresh in your mind, you can detail out the pros, detail out the cons, and see if there's anything you missed. Ask yourself:

Do they match the strengths

Going into this interview, you should have had a crystal clear idea of the skills and strengths you were looking for. As you went through your conversation, did you get a good sense of how many of those skills they had, and at what level? Now is the time to fill out the scorecard you designed, and be really honest with yourself about how they showed up.

Are there any red flags

In the course of the interview, did anything pop up that seemed off, or surprised you in a weird way. While keeping bias in mind, take a minute to think, "What was it about what they said that struck me?" "Why did it give me pause?" Don't make any snap judgments, but do take your reactions seriously.

Dave Hoffer told me about the time he had a candidate functionally talk his way out of a job, and he was glad he was looking out for the red flags:

> "At McKinsey, I was interviewing someone for a design role, and this one candidate seemed decent. Checked all the boxes. Had the right qualifications. Fit the job description.
>
> I asked him, 'tell me about your typical day,' and his response really tanked his interview.
>
> He said, 'I get up at 7am. I grab a quick breakfast, do a quick workout. Then I get into emails for my side hustle. I can knock out a lot and be ready to go, ready to work at 9am. Then I work. At 5 I come back and continue emailing and working on my side hustle until it's time to go to bed.'
>
> He went into so many details about his side hustle, about all the things he was working on. And it was clear that's what he was really into: and it wasn't the 9-5 of the design work. And while some places are 9-5, McKinsey didn't work that way. If you were on a project, you were working, especially if you were on a deadline. The focus needed to be on the work, and we didn't have time or energy to have a whole other job. And that's what it sounded like this guy had.
>
> Essentially, this particular job would have demanded more

than he was able to give, so I knew right then and there that he wasn't a good fit."

-Dave Hoffer, Designer

In the end, it's up to you, which is good and bad. As a hiring manager, you're the person best suited to determine if a candidate meets enough of the criteria to move forward. On the other hand, you might feel like there are some unknowns still left to explore. If you're on the fence, have a chat with the recruiter to see if they have the same concerns or feedback. They can validate your hunches, or have a different take you didn't consider. What you want to avoid is moving a candidate through because you simply don't know, and you want the panel to decide. This isn't fair to the panel or to the candidate. Moving them forward in the process is an overt endorsement, and they should have your demonstrable support.

Use your (informed) instinct, rely on your scorecard, and be honest with yourself, and the candidate, either way.

Takeaways

Practice good interview etiquette

Be present. Be fair. Take notes. Be reassuring. Be kind. And be on time.

Design your own interview

Build a strong, repeatable hiring manager protocol that gets you what you need, every time.

Make it conversational

Get to know the candidate as comfortably as possible, and make it a conversation where they get to know you as much as you get to know them. Leave room for improvisation!

CHAPTER SIX

Don't go it alone: putting together and prepping your panel

While much of the interview process is done on your own, there will come a time in your process when it's time to call in for additional help, insight, and expertise. This means putting together your panel of cross-functional friends to get different takes on your candidate, and hopefully build consensus to make a hire. Granted, it doesn't always go so seamlessly: people may be looking for different things, have different reads, or prioritize different strengths. Plus, they'll be carrying in their own biases into the process. So many variables and places for things to go sideways! That's why it's crucial to assemble your panel with intention, with excellent preparation, and to facilitate the discussion to make sure you're getting an informed, useful opinion (even if it's not a consensus). Let's get into it.

Avengers: assemble!

For panel interviews, you're not just looking for people that will agree with you, or people who all have the same opinion. What you're looking for is a diverse set of folks, ideally ones who will work with this candidate. 3-4 people is plenty, especially if you're going to do a panel interview followed by 1:1s.

Panel-building is a strategic exercise. Beyond just getting someone to ask questions and take notes, you're also setting the potential hire up for success from the first conversation. You're getting them to meet the people they'd be working with most closely, or people who can give them an informed perspective on what it's like to work as a Designer at your company. Depending on the role, the panel might look like:

All the same discipline: just Content Design, just Designers, just Researchers

If you're hiring a very senior practitioner and you want to get a well-rounded assessment of craft, you might assemble your panel from a range of people with roughly the same role. This might be great if you're hiring a specialist (taxonomist, prototyper, etc), and they'll mostly be working with other Content Designers, Designers, or Researchers.

Cross-functional mix: a Designer/Content Designer, a PM, a Researcher
If you're hiring someone into a particular team with a gap, it may make sense for the panel to be made up of those people. This way they are on board and bought in with the candidate, vs. having a brand new person plopped into the team.

Leads/directs: hiring a new manager
If you're hiring a new manager to the team, you may want to have the panel be a mix of people they'll be managing and people they'll be peers with. Coming in as a new manager is a tough job, so making sure the team is engaged in bringing in that person is crucial to make sure the candidate is a good fit.

Strategic selection
At the top, I said you'd be assembling a crew of your cross-functional friends. That's mostly true, but once in awhile, it's good to recruit your work nemesis as well. They don't have to be your serious nemesis, but maybe it's the person who has a tendency to undermine what you do, question your decisions, and generally make your job a bit harder. They might come in hot, have strong opinions, and seek to undo all your good work. You know who I'm talking about. I bet you're picturing them right now.

If your work nemesis is going to be working closely with this hire, have a hand in their onboarding, or will be collaborating with them in any meaningful way, it's a good idea to get their opinion from the start, and listen to their opinions through the process. You'll want them bought in on the hire, especially if you need them to be supportive once the candidate is on board.

This can be tough. I've had to pass on candidates I really believed in, just because my work nemesis didn't share my opinion. I needed them bought in, because the two would have to work together. It was a tough call, but it was the right one: that candidate wouldn't have had a fair start. They would have to prove themselves even more than normal, and the nemesis would have been looking for a reason to hate on them.

In that instance, we did find a candidate we both believed in. Not only was it a better start for the candidate, but it was a good moment of relationship repair for me and the work nemesis. We built trust through the process, and because I listened to their opinion and valued it.

Prepare your panel!

Your panel is set, maybe you're already putting calendar holds on the books for an interview, now's the time to get your interview guide all set up! A little preparation goes a long way in making sure your panelists are getting the information both you and they need to make a hiring recommendation. While you want to leave some room for rapport and vibes, you also want to make sure your panelists have a bit of structure to follow. This ensures they're assessing for the right strengths, experience and expertise you're looking for in a given candidate. To do this, you'll write an interview guide.

Panelists will often sit in a group presentation, then break off into 1:1s. Your interview guide should cover both portions of the interview process.

Setting up the role

The interview guide is going to have a lot in common with your job description. You want to start with a link to the JD, plus a summary of what you're looking for. Include the job title, team, and anything else the interviewer should know about the role. This might look like:

- Domain expertise you're looking for
- Specific skills that are must-have/nice-to-have

- Who they'll be working with
- Anything else relevant to this particular role

Remember those documents we created in Chapter 1? They're back, baby. Create a version of your Assessment Criteria for your panel to use. They'll be considering the candidate for all the "Have" skills, as well as how advanced they are. They can use this as a scorecard to determine if the candidate they're talking to matches the core criteria for the role.

Prepping for presentations

For the presentation section, make sure you include what the presentation prompt was that was given to the candidate. You can also tie it back to the strengths you're looking for, or what you're looking for specifically. You'll also want to use the same scorecard you've been using all along.

For example:
We've asked the candidate to prepare a presentation telling a little bit about their design journey, plus two case studies. We've asked for two contrasting case studies that highlight cross-functional collaboration, experience with style guides and/or internationalization, as well as any experience they may have working with non-profits.

You can give your panelists a few assessment directions to anchor on, or let them take free-form notes (or both). The assessment directions are entirely up to you, and might vary from panelist to panelist, depending on what opinion you're looking to elicit from them.

For example:
Design craft. Does the quality of the work match your expectations? Is it consistent and clean, free from errors, typos, or mistakes? Is it understandable?

Design articulation. Does the candidate sufficiently explain or justify their choices? Do they explain the inputs and constraints, then successfully balance them?

Cross-functional experience. Does the candidate display understanding of how other functions work and how they've collaborated with them? Can they speak to conflict or overcoming differences of opinion?

Domain expertise. Does this candidate have facility and understanding with X domain expertise? Would you consider them an expert?

Create a single template that works for everyone, so you're comparing similarly formatted feedback when it's time to assess. You can set this up in Greenhouse (or whatever tool your company is using), or a simple doc.

1:1 interview guide

Now that your panelists have been through the presentation, you'll want to give them some light structure for their 1:1 interview. If you're asking them to conduct a 30-minute interview, you don't want to over-structure it. Don't want to be too prescriptive here: allow time and space for the interviewer to design the conversation the way they'd like. They should have time to answer any specific questions that came up to them during the panel presentation, and make sure they're leaving time at the end for any questions the candidate has.

The 1:1 guide might look like:

- 5 mins: introduce yourself: what you do here, how long you've been here, where you live (if you'd like).

- 10 mins: any follow-up questions you have from the presentation. This might look like: questions about a particular design decision, anything you found confusing or would like more context on, something you want to dig deeper on
- 10 mins: pick 1-2 questions from the interview question bank
- 5 mins: allow time for candidate questions

Interview question bank

Your company/department might already have a list of approved questions, and if so, pull from there. If you're designing your own, many of the most useful questions are ones that elicit a story or specific experience, that highlight a skill or strength, or invoke particular domain knowledge. This isn't a time for "gotcha" questions or insidious tricky impossible questions. Leave the "how many ping-pong balls fit in a school bus" to Google lore. Instead, prep your panelists with well-structured questions that provide useful insight into the candidate.

"Tell me about a time when..."

Such a useful construct! This question format is at once open-ended and specific. It leaves room for interpretation and sets the candidate up to tell their own story, in their own words. You can finish the question in any number of ways, depending on what you need to learn:

Tell me about a time when you had to balance user and business needs

Tell me about a time when you used research to inform your design decisions

Tell me about a time when you set out to acquire a new skill

Tell me about a time when you overcame conflict with a coworker

Tell me about a time when you disagreed with your manager

Write the questions that speak to the aspects of the candidate you're looking for, and mix the questions up across the panelists. Ideally, you'd like to have the candidate have very different conversations from panelist to panelist (vs. them telling the same anecdotes over and over again).

Scoring and structure

Finally, for the interview guide, you want to prepare the panelist to give useful feedback and be able to have as much of an unbiased conversation as possible at the end. In addition to the scorecard, I ask my panelists to summarize their feedback in the following way:

Pros. What makes this candidate a great fit? What are their strengths and skills? Why would they thrive here?

Cons. What concerns or reservations do you have? Any open questions?

Hiring decision. Strong no hire/No hire/Hire/Strong yes hire

This straightforward rubric gives the panelists something to anchor on, and structures the hire/no-hire conversation you'll have later. Ask the panelists to keep their feedback confidential until the debrief: strong opinions can sway other people before you have a chance to process all the information.

Gratitude

Interviewing is work. Interviewing takes time. Interviewing can be really frustrating when you spend a lot of time on it and a candidate isn't hired. Throughout the process, make sure you're respecting your panelists' time, giving them thanks for their contributions, and letting them know their work matters. It goes a long way!

Conducting the panel interview

It's interview day! Your candidate is set, the panelists are ready. Let's do this thing.

Get everyone on the same page

In the interview guide and in the calendar invite, add some key instructions and best practices for interviewing, as well as expectations. Encourage your panelists to have their cameras on, to not multitask, and to focus on the task at hand. Ask them to take notes and actively listen: their time and opinion is important, and you want to make sure every minute counts.

Set up the structure

Once everyone is in the room (virtual or physical), kick off the panel by setting some expectations. This might look like structure, context, and letting people know if you plan to have questions at the end or if people should reserve their questions for the 1:1. If the 1:1s are happening directly after, it might be good to have the questions reserved for those conversations. If the 1:1s are another day, then follow-up questions when the material is best is probably better for the candidate and for the interviewer.

Do a super quick round of intros

Ask the panelists to introduce themselves, their title, and maybe how long they've been at the company.

Hand over the mic

While the candidate is talking, take notes, listen closely, and keep your interview guide nearby. Write down any questions you might have as they come up (and keep listening in case they answer those questions in the course of the presentation). As much as is natural, be a warm and welcoming active listener. Panel presentations can be super intimidating!

Allow time for questions (optional)

Again, depending on when the 1:1s are, you may want to hold off on having the panelists ask questions. That said, if the questions are specifically about the case studies and might be asked by multiple people, then leave the floor open. This case usually happens in a more homogenous panel (all Content Designers, all Designers, all Researchers).

Help the candidate by keeping time

If you see the clock running out, you can absolutely help the candidate by giving them a time check. Or if a panelists' discussion or question is taking a longer-than-expected time, you have the right to tactfully end the discussion and encourage the interview to move on.

Wrap up, move on

At the end, thank everyone for their time and attention, and thank the candidate for their work!

Getting the band together

After the panel interviews and 1:1's, it's time to gather the team together to decide: go or no-go? No matter if you or the recruiter is leading this part of the process, it's time once again to be honest, to check your biases, and to be realistic about how this person's strengths match up with what you're looking for.

First things first: collect the data

Before you call everyone together to have a chat about the candidate, you can ask them to submit their feedback directly to you (or in a feedback tool like Greenhouse). Keep the results to yourself, so the panel isn't swayed. You'll check for hire/no hire decisions, read through the pros and cons, and track any patterns you see emerging. Even if it's all "strong no hires" or "strong yes hires" across the board, don't give in to the temptation to cancel the debrief. People may still want an opportunity to express their excitement (or reservations), and the final meeting can give people a sense of finality to that candidate either way.

Debrief time

In order to keep biases in check, allow everyone equal time to give feedback, and keep everything as fair as possible for everyone, I recommend a really structured debrief in four steps:

1. Ask for bias

   Give the panelists an opportunity to declare any biases they might have. This might look like knowing the person, working at the same company they did, having people in common, going to the same college, or anything else that might sway an opinion. This also could be a bias against them because they worked at a certain company, or have a certain background.

2. Get the pros

   One by one, without revealing a hiring decision, ask each panelist to tell everyone what the candidate's strengths were, what stood out as positive, and what the candidate did well. It's ok if these get a little redundant the more people go.

3. Get the cons

   Same on the flip side. One by one, ask the panelists to declare what reservations they have, what misses or gaps they saw, or anything else that might keep them from a "hire" decision. Same goes here: the last person might just say "I agree with everything everyone else said."

4. Speak to the hiring decision
   At this point, it should be fairly obvious if the team is feeling hire/no hire, though that isn't always the case. I've been on a panel with three people who had a tepid "hire" recommendation, but then another person came in with a strong "no hire" take. Through the course of the discussion, and the outlier articulating the potential weaknesses, the rest of the panel came over to the "no hire" camp. I've seen the very opposite happen too. Let people have their say, address reservations, but the call, most likely, will be up to you (no pressure. JK all the pressure).

Beware the "culture fit" trap

Hiring isn't black and white. You get a slim view of an entire person, and need to make a decision based on what they present. Beyond the core skills and strengths, there's also vibes, which is where things get exceedingly tricky. Can a person *just* have the skills to do the design work? Sure. But design isn't done in a vacuum. Work is an inherently collaborative effort. At once the question, "Do I want to work with them" is very valid and wholly irrelevant. So how do you answer it without falling into your biases or giving into your gut (which is made of bias, btw).

When you hear yourself or a panelist bring up "culture fit," then it's time to gently question: what does that mean? Is this about working at a big company, or working at a start-up? Is this about being soft-spoken vs. being somewhat brash? Is this about wanting to work with people that share the same values, background, or experience as you do? Is that good? Or does working in design mean seeking different perspectives, which come from different backgrounds, and different points-of-view?

So now you have all the data you need to make a decision. Hire or no hire? Keep the interview ball rolling or make an offer? Either way, be very gracious, thank your panel profusely, and then continue on with tempered confidence.

Takeaways

Assemble your team intentionally

Interviewing is a team sport, and choosing your panel is a strategic exercise. Make sure the right people are in the room.

Prepare your documentation in detail

Give panelists a great guide so they understand the strengths and skills you're looking for. Leave them room to make it their own, but keep the scoring protocol the same.

Combat bias clearly

Bias is big in discussions. Make sure you're getting ahead of it respectfully and overtly.

CHAPTER SEVEN

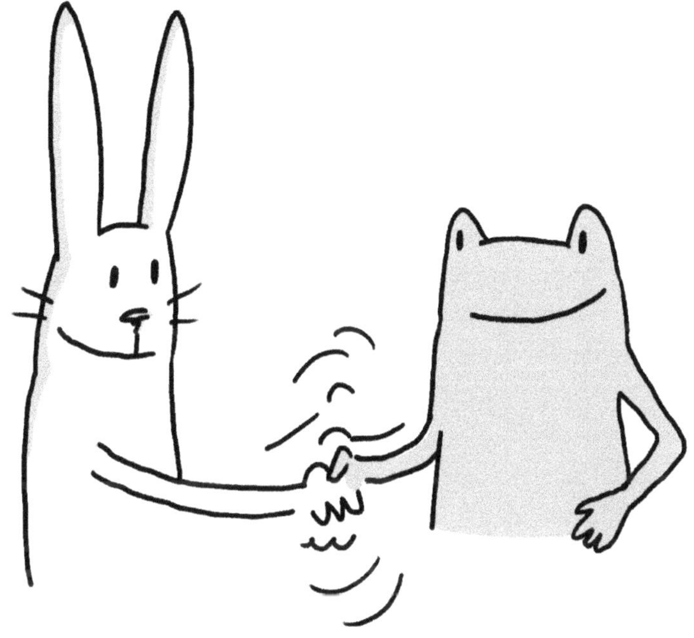

Putting a ring on it (maybe)

The screening, the hiring manager interview, the panel presentation, the 1:1s. They're all in your rearview mirror. You should have enough info to go on at this point, but maybe, just maybe, there's something you're still on the fence about. Here's how to navigate those particular waters.

Falling in love too easily

When my then-boyfriend-now-husband and I were moving in together, we went through the arduous exercise of looking for an apartment in San Francisco. With two cats, a recently acquired baby grand piano, and a modest budget, I was sure we'd have a hard time finding anything. That said, I also love old buildings in SF and was excited to apartment-hunt and see how charming of a place we could find.

The first place we saw, I was sure it was IT. Soaring ceilings, right in the Mission across from a notorious ice cream shop, a big kitchen, and the outside was painted a funky purple. I was giddy looking in every room. The ceiling medallions! Pocket doors! I was ready to write a deposit check right there. Then my then-boyfriend-now-husband pointed to the gigantic water heater taking up a third of the kitchen. The closet doors that weren't doors but curtains. "And it's the color of Grimace from McDonalds." He had a point. He had three points. And I was very aware that I am too quick to fall in love with crappy apartments.

Eager to see the good in the situation, I can explain away any shortcomings (we can put a screen around the water heater! We can get cool beaded curtains for the closets! People will be able to find our place so easily!). For me, it's crucial that I really pause, listen to the other opinions and be realistic, and understand what is and isn't a dealbreaker.

> "I always believe in the capabilities of people I talk to. But I'm also honest if those capabilities don't match with what a given team needs."
> -Margie Levinson, Content Design Leader

Same goes for considering candidates. This is the time to ask yourself:

- Am I chasing the dragon when I saw this candidate on paper and thought, "This is the one?"
- Have they sufficiently demonstrated they possess the qualities outlined in your must-haves?
- Is the team bought in, and would they be excited to work with them?
- Will they be able to do the job and meet the requirements your team needs right this moment?

Be honest, be real, give yourself time to think about it.

> "If you have two candidates in final rounds, and you have one with less experience but has demonstrated more passion for the role, I always advise to go for the one with passion for the role."
> -Christina (Maz) Mazurowski, Product Recruitment at Datadog

But also, beware of quick dismissals

Maybe they said a weird thing. Maybe something came up in one of the interviews that felt like a red (or yellow) flag. Maybe they used an outmoded term and you're mentally dinging them in your head for that. This is also a time to interrogate those reservations, and see how they stack up to your must-haves.

This is the time to ask yourself:

- Did anything happen that indicates they couldn't do this job?
- Is one of the lacking skills, strengths or other criteria one of your must-haves, or was it a nice-to-have?
- Is the weakness you perceived coachable?
- Did someone on the panel have a very strong case for or against this candidate?

Maybe the reason you want to say no isn't a sufficient reason at all, and it is worth making an offer. Also, you're very much within your rights to have one more conversation with any given candidate.

Make it quick, make it straightforward, and give yourself an opportunity to assuage your doubts (and give them a chance to ask any lingering questions they might have).

> "I was brought in a candidate that was also on the cusp, but was flagged for being 'too passive.' I had a follow-up interview with them, and I was really direct and asked them about it. They said, 'I've been [a member of a protected group] my whole life. I've had to fight for myself from the beginning.' I took them on, and they ended up being so good, so strong. I sometimes thought we were weeding out people for the wrong reasons, making decisions based on our projection, not the individual's true skills and capabilities."
> -Frank Marquardt, Head of Content Design, Yahoo

About that coachable thing

In the course of an interview process, you may find that a candidate is weak in one particular area, and you think "it's coachable!" That might be presentation skills, speaking to craft, or potentially core skills like writing or designing. You may be thinking, "I'm open to hiring them, and coaching them on this thing."

It's time to be honest again.

If you're considering a coachable candidate, ask yourself:

- What is the skill that needs coaching, and who is going to do it?
- Does that person have the capacity to mentor in this particular way?
- Is this a skill the candidate needs from day one, or can it wait?
- What if they are unable to grow in this area? Are they still a good hire?

This is not to say "Don't hire someone who you see as needing coaching." Not at all. But just be honest about what you need, what this candidate's capacity is, and if they're really truly the right person for this job, right now. Because you might be falling into....

The sunk-cost fallacy trap. You have spent so much time on this job opening. You convinced the headcount to be opened, you wrote the job description, this candidate made it through the resume review, the screening, your interview, the panel, the 1:1s. They're so close! But close may not be it. You don't want to go back to square one, but you may have to. If this is a crucial role, if this person really needs to succeed on their own, if this hire is going to reflect back on you, then it really does need to be right. It's not only fair to you, it's fair to the candidate as well. You want a good fit. Maybe not a perfect fit, but somewhere in the neighborhood. You can keep looking if you need to. It's ok.

It's a hard line to draw: the candidate should really be at their very best in an interview. This setting is where they should be shining and impressing. That said, interviewing makes people really nervous! So if there's odd behavior you're seeing, it might be that, or it might be them. I know. It's so hard.

But also, sometimes it's not, and it's totally ok to be exceedingly excited about a candidate. And when you are...

OMG OFFER TIME!

Also, you might not have any of these questions! You might have just found the perfect candidate that ticks all the boxes, that the team is genuinely excited about, that has knocked everyone's collective socks off. It's ok to be excited! It's ok to share that excitement with the team, and more importantly, it's ok to share that excitement with the candidate themself!

Making an offer is usually the time when you deputize the recruiter to work out all the details like salary, benefits, start date and all those other negotiations. Let them do their thing (and don't be put off if you hear your candidate is negotiating fiercely. They should be!). While all that is being worked out, reach out to the candidate, shoot them a note of reasonable enthusiasm and heartfelt excitement. Offer your availability for any open questions about the work, the team, the company, what have you. You can also encourage the panelists to reach out to the candidate as well with the same direction. Your candidate might be on the fence, and those entreaties might just push them over the edge.

I had been contracting at Lyft for about six months, and it was time for them to either put a ring on it or for me to go elsewhere. I was in late-stage interviews with another company that was at once very intriguing and also full of red flags. In the course of making a decision, I got more than a few Slack messages from the Design Leads, hoping I would stay, clearly excited about the prospect. While the other offer was really interesting, it was these messages that tipped the scale for me. A little note goes a long way.

Keep that happy momentum going

First, congrats to you! Hiring is a huge, often unseen lift of being in design. It takes a lot of work, a lot of time, and very few people take the time to learn how to do it right (someone should write a book about that. Oh wait!). So well done. Seriously. It's a big deal. You're a job creator. You gave someone that new-job feeling. I'm proud of you.

So keep that good thing going. In that lull between offer acceptance and first day, take the time to set your candidate new hire up for success. Take time to make a really good onboarding doc. Find some company swag to send them. Set up a team lunch for them their first week. Sort out how you're going to introduce them to the team, and let everyone know when their first day is coming up. It's an exciting time: for you, for the team, and for your awesome new hire.

Good job.

Takeaways

Take your candidates for who they are
If there were any red flags along the way, consider that in this setting, this should be the candidates very best version of themselves. Those red flags may only get redder.

Don't fall for sunk-cost
Be really honest with yourself if this candidate is truly the right fit for a job: it's easy to think about the time you've spent, how much the work needs to get done. Having the wrong person in the job will just mean more work down the line.

Celebrate the win, damn it
Being able to give someone that "I-just-got-a-job-offer" feeling is pretty exciting. Celebrate the win and keep the good momentum going with a note from you and from the team.

Resources

Books

If you've got room on your bookshelf for more books, these are some of the professional books and workbooks that have stood out to me. Most are recent, but there are some older books about work that still resonate with me.

Hire with your Head, Lou Adler
Design the Life You Love, by Ayse Birsel
Gig: Americans Talk About their Jobs, edited by John Bowe (2009)
A Designer's Guide to Interviewing, by Tanner Christiansen
Interview Hero, by Angela Guido
Conversational Design, by Erika Hall
Just Enough Research, by Erika Hall
Creating a Successful Graphic Design Portfolio, by Irina Lee

Design is a Job, by Mike Monteiro
Burnout: The Secret to Unlocking the Stress Cycle, by Emily Nagoski and Amelia Nagoski
Creative Hustle, by Olatunde Sobomehin
Working: People Talk About What They Do All Day, by Studs Terkel (1974)
Never Search Alone: The Job-Seeker's Playbook, by Phyl Terry
How to Do Nothing: Resisting the Attention Economy, by Jenny Odell
The First 90 Days, Michael D. Watkins
Getting to Yes, Ury, et al. (1980, but there are newer editions)
Taking the Work out of Networking, by Karen Wickre
The Making of a Manager, Julie Zhuo

Good people to follow

A bunch of great people I've come across, who often post great advice on the various socials. We're putting this in print, so let's just hope no one gets canceled. That's to say, putting them in the resource section isn't an endorsement for everything they do.

Lou Adler
Malaika Carpenter

Erika Hall
Andy Healy
Jessica Hirch
Shannon Leahy
Farai Madzima
Debbie Millman
Mike Monteiro
Robin Rendle
Jared Spool
David Dylan Thomas
Kat Vellos
Candi Williams
Harrison Wheeler
Leslie Yang

References

Much of this book came out of personal experiences and interviews with experts, novices, and everyone in between. Here are some additional references, per chapter, that I drew from.

Designing Interviews

Chapter 1: Designing the design job

Jared Spool, "UX Hiring: The Performance Profile is a Game Changer"
medium.com/creating-a-ux-strategy-playbook/ux-hiring-the-performance-profile-is-a-game-changer-1dd1b13698ad

Chapter 4: Reading resumes and decoding portfolios

Oliver Lindberg, "Designing for Unconscious Biases, an interview with David Dylan Thomas"
medium.com/ux-and-front-end-interviews/designing-for-unconscious-biases-an-interview-with-david-dylan-thomas-8ba78a31208b

David Dylan Thomas, "Design for Cognitive Bias"

Dan Pontefract, "Why Indeed's View on Career Decline is So Wrong"
www.forbes.com/sites/danpontefract/2024/09/03/why-indeeds-view-on-career-decline-is-so-wrong

Interviewing in Design

Chapter 1: What's in a job?

www.therapistaid.com/therapy-worksheet/your-wisest-self

Lou Adler, "A Great Career Move is Not About the Money"
www.linkedin.com/pulse/how-i-hire-great-career-move-money-lou-adler

Chapter 2: Setting up your search

"Never Search Alone," phyl.org

Chapter 3: Artifacts of a search: resumes, case studies and sites

Leslie Yang, "What a Hiring Manager Looks for in Product Design Portfolios and Presentations"
leslieyang.substack.com/p/what-a-hiring-manager-looks-for-in

Andy Healey, "How to get a job with Shopify UX"
medium.com/shopify-ux/how-to-get-a-job-with-shopify-ux-fc07161bb982

Chapter 5: Everything before the interview
"Interview Hero," by Angela Guido

Ben George, "Why you should say no to take-home exercises"
bytes.referralcandy.com/why-you-should-say-no-to-take-home-exercises-3b9a4b4c8e0d

Chapter 7: After the interview: knowing your worth through offers (and everything else)
"Coping with Ghosting," Podcast, Gretta Perlmutter

"The Ultimate Guide to Salary Negotiation for Designers," Linn Vizard
xd.adobe.com/ideas/career-tips/ultimate-guide-salary-negotiation-designers/

Acknowledgments

To Matthew Brinegar, my in-house counsel, thank you for your support, for bringing me cats, and encouraging me every step of the way. I like you the most.

To Josh Silverman, cheerleader, designer, and partner in this book. I couldn't have done this without you.

To Sharina Wunderink, an incredible and insightful editor who gave structure to my chapters and insight to my blind spots.

To Jared Spool, who generously offered expertise, experience and brilliant insight to the work. Your support means so much.

To Betsy Streeter, for bringing humanity to this work with your amazing illustrations.

To Jenny Wapner, for everything.

To Justin Maxwell, with whom I've been trading advice for years now. See you on Tuesday (or the Tuesday after).

To Erika Hall and Lisa Maria Marquis, if not for that short walk from the last Confab to the afterparty, this book wouldn't be a thing. Thank you/damn you.

To Kristina Halvorson, Margot Bloomstein, and Torrey Podmajersky. Thank you for being early readers and staunch supporters. Your words gave this work life!

To everyone I interviewed for the book: Margie Levinson, Frank Marquardt, Andy Welfle, Rob Surrency, Chelsea Larsson, Dave Hoffer, Reina Belardes, Nathan Falstreau, Amy Lipner, Josie Jeffries, Maz Murkowski, Leslie Forman, Taylor Howard, Joel Soloman, Chase Bucklew-Geddes, and probably more!

To anyone who pitched in with design support, like Jason Cosper and Conor Buckley, plus all the people on the various and sundry Slacks.

To everyone I've interviewed to get a job or to give a job.

Thank you.

Margo Stern is a Staff Content Designer living and working in San Francisco. After spending a decade in advertising as a copywriter, tech scooped her up and made a Content Designer out of her. She's worked as a manager and IC at Google, Twitter, Facebook, and Peloton (and more!). When she's not writing, you can find her at the boxing gym or the pool, or traveling the world with her very patient husband.

Image: Lisa Keating

www.ingramcontent.com/pod-product-compliance
Lightning Source LLC
Chambersburg PA
CBHW040923210326
41597CB00030B/5160

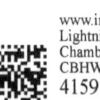

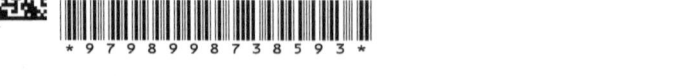

* 9 7 9 8 9 9 8 7 3 8 5 9 3 *

GOOD JOB

Interviewing in Design

(for the candidate)

First edition. Published by Sternly Worded, San Francisco, CA, USA

ISBN 979-8-9987385-9-3

Cover and text design by Josh Silverman.

Body serif typeface: Brix Slab. Body and header sans typeface: Koga Sans.

Illustrations by Betsy Streeter.

Contents

Foreword

Torrey Podmajersky

President of Catbird Content

My grandparents had expectations that "good" companies would nurture employee's careers, and eventually say goodbye at a retirement party after 50 years of dedicated service. "Treat them well, and they'll treat you well."

That was the point of getting a college degree, they told me: get a job at a good company, and it would be my constant companion for 40-60 hours per week for the rest of my life. But by the time I went to college, that "promise" was a threadbare fiction.

Companies aren't our friends. We are in an era of extraordinary profits, monopolization, and wealth inequality in most of the companies where UX professionals seek jobs. These businesses are playing a complex game with investment capital, hype cycles, and stock valuations. This can create great excitement for employees, because the problems are always new. But it is also fundamentally unstable: these companies aren't focused on old-school business fundamentals of "making products people like" and "investing in employees who create value."

The way our economy is structured, we need those jobs. But instead of interviewing with and staying with one company, having our careers nurtured and grown over decades, it's more common to need a new employer every few years. So what do we do? We go get those jobs, using the methods this book provides.

We don't assume that it's obvious how impressive we are, so we learn to strut so that people can admire exactly the kind of powerful, creative, adaptable person we are. We don't passively accept the first job that comes along, we go out and hunt for the right job for us. We don't accept the first salary offer we get, we negotiate for more.

But we're not just solo hunters, alone in the wilderness. Margo reminds us that we're in this job search for ourselves, but also for others.

I hate bragging, but I'm proud of the difference I've made for people and organizations. When one of us represents the impact of their UX work well, we're improving that hiring team's understanding and ability to articulate UX impact, too.

I hate negotiating, but I know that starting salaries are the first place we teach an organization the value of what we're worth. When one of us negotiates a higher salary, we're improving salaries for the next UX pros hired, too.

I hate looking for a job, but life is too short to suffer more than we can avoid. When one of us has the privilege to leave a bad team or situation, we're giving that team reasons to improve before hiring their next UX pro, too.

This book is the plucky, fierce friend that can remind you to straighten up, get down to work, and avoid the tempting pitfalls that seem to lurk everywhere in the job seeking process. Margo is here for

us and includes the vital advice to find job-search buddies. By working together, we make all of these individual UX jobs into a sustainable discipline.

That's why I'm depending on you to get the next fantastic job for you. I believe you can do it. Onward, job seeker!

P.S. It wasn't until I became a manager that I really learned how to represent myself and my work. I didn't understand what the managers were going through, and how much pressure they're under to find exactly the right person to work with. Find out what they're going through by reading the other side of this book, and start to empathize with them! Your future manager is working hard to try to find you right now.

CHAPTER ONE

What's in a job?

So you've decided to look for a job in design. Congratulations! This is the first step on an exciting journey to a new life and a new you.

Oof.

Can you imagine?

I mean, some people might feel like this sometimes: enlivened by opportunity, excited for all that's to come. And that feeling very well may come along: namely with that "woo they offered me the job!" feeling. But we're keeping it 100 around here, and know that the job search isn't always the most thrilling thing to do. But, there are ways to make it suck a whole lot less. We'll talk through how being curious,

being focused, and being honest (and gentle) with yourself can make the job-searching experience a whole lot less awful.

But before we even get to that, maybe we should ask: what even is a job though?

From your first job out of school to starting a search after your third layoff in a row, job searching can be exciting, exhausting, and everything in between. It's a lot. So before we start constructing our resumes and building out portfolios, we can start by considering: beyond the obvious ($), why even have a job in the first place, and how do careers get built?

Every career is different. Every path is different.

There's a point in every naming exercise where someone asks the question: does this even need a name? And I think that line of inquiry is good here. Do I really need a job? And what does it mean anyway? What is a career path?

Mine started with a pragmatic degree in Russian Literature and Language, which naturally led to a first career as an advertising copywriter. After making commercials for caffeinated beverages and videogames, I was fortunate enough to get picked up at Google for my second career, where I learned on the job about being a Content Strategist. Since then I've built and led teams. I've been an Individual Contributor (IC). I've been freelance, I've been full-time. I've been at big companies and I've been at start-ups. I even took a break from all of it by working in a cheese store for three months.

Every step of my career path has been informed by so many choices and factors: what I thought was meaningful to me, how I defined

success, my values, my experience. Plus all those other things I had no control over: who was hiring (and for what level), the job market, the mysteries of the economy. Part of getting into your job search isn't just imagining a career path, but understanding what's driving you: is it just about money (fine!), or about some other kind of fulfillment? What might you compromise on and what is something that's a non-starter?

There's not just one way to have a successful career in design. What's more, your definition of success might change as your career path takes shape.

And while this book biases towards preparing for a Big Interview for a Big Full-Time Job with Big Benefits, I'll also invite you to open up your definition of what a dream job looks like. So before we start getting into portfolios and resumes, interview questions and navigating offers, let's consider your values.

Before you start your search, define your values

You are a person in the world. You are a person, interacting with other people. You are a person with history, emotions, relationships and ethics that shape how you move through the world. These are your values, and they're worth defining.

Values are different to each person, and entirely personal. They're informed by your experience, your background, and what you define as important to you.

Take a look at some sample values, and see how you react to them. Do you agree? Do you disagree? Try saying them out loud. You'll likely have a visceral reaction to them: a big yes or a big ick.

These are sample values. Try saying them out loud:
Growing my skills and experience with every job
Making as much money as I can
Making the world a better place
Ensuring people are safe and secure
Doing work with integrity and morality
Doing whatever it takes to innovate

Which of these feel right to you? Which of these don't exactly fit? These kinds of questions and statements may inform how you define your values as a worker and as a designer.

A common therapy exercise is to ask yourself a series of introspective questions that get at defining your values. We do this so we can go into big life choices with our eyes wide open, being clear on what we can compromise on and what we can't. When we find ourselves in situations that don't align with our values, it saps our energy, feels off, and makes us not want to continue.

So let's ask ourselves these questions:

- Looking back, what accomplishments or experiences have mattered the most to you?
- How do you hope your loved ones will remember you?
- What advice would you give your younger self?
- Based on that advice, what values are important to you now?
- How do the career goals you have in mind align with those values?

The answers to these may change over time, but many will stay the same. For me, my values lie in doing work that creates safer experiences, that prioritizes people and empathy, that centers human experience. I've learned I no longer value a big title, but I do value time to pursue non-work things, like music, swimming, and watching Below Deck with one or two cats on my lap.

Next, let's consider how the values you define inform how you shape your career.

Non-linear career paths are cool

Sometimes I'll meet a new, very junior hire, and find out that they came to the company straight out of college, where they studied UX Design. On one hand, I think it's cool that you can study UX Design in college, on the other hand, it strikes me as a bit of a missed opportunity. I learned so much as I was figuring it out: working at a newspaper, answering phones at an ad agency, finding out what a copywriter was, being a cater-waiter, being freelance, full-time, and everything in between.

Each step in my career path came with valuable lessons and experience. I learned about where I thrived and where I failed. I learned how burnout can lead to rash decisions (like working at that cheese shop because I was done with advertising). I learned what motivates me (working in integrity and accessibility) and what bores me (growth initiatives and tools). The twists in the path itself inform the journey and help clarify values and priorities.

If you find yourself on a non-linear path, there are some very good reasons to enjoy the exploration. If you're on a straight path and have worry about straying, know that there are some really great reasons for a detour.

Every experience is good experience

> "Regrets, I've had a few
> But then again, too few to mention..."
> -Frank Sinatra singing *My Way*

Any given career is going to be met with a few highs, and some pretty spectacular lows. I assure you, just about every person you perceive as impossibly successful has been fired, given harsh feedback, resigned a position they thought was going to change their lives. But there's good reason to live through those experiences.

A few of the jobs I've expected didn't turn out how I thought they would be. A start-up that promised to be a rocket ship that flamed out with spectacular toxicity. A title I pursued doggedly at a company I thought I loved only to be shown the door. And even though these experiences were painful in their own way, I believe, without cynicism or sugarcoating that I really learned a lot.

Each of these steps on my career path clarified my values and shaped the way I tell my story. Every experience is good experience, because it helps define what matters most to you. So if you find a job that aligns with some of your values, but may not align with your so-called "career goals," see what you might compromise on. Consider the temp-to-perm. Take a risk on a start-up if it seems interesting. Find out what it's like to work for a brand you admire. You might learn something.

Sometimes you really need a break

> "You need time and distance to understand what your story is really about. It took me a full year after leaving one job to have enough perspective to see, to look more broadly at the narrative of my career."
> -Leslie Forman, Professor of Storytelling at California College of the Arts

I'd been working in advertising for a decade, and my last shop was not a good fit. I was working on products I couldn't summon any genuine interest in, with a nemesis for a work partner. I was not

motivated, and I was pretty unsupported by the agency. I was a resource, and I wasn't delivering. It wasn't great for anyone, and they fired me. I couldn't fathom applying to be another copywriter somewhere, so I took a break to go work at a cheese store (I promise this is the last time I'll mention it). I thought cheese mongering was going to be an awesome new career: I'd talk about cheese all day, maybe find time to do some freelancing on the side just to keep up my chops. Three months later, I was too exhausted from being on my feet making sandwiches to consider doing freelance work. I found that I was introducing myself as someone "who works at a cheese shop, but I'm really a writer." Finally, when cutting an avocado with the wrong knife sent me to the ER, I realized I'd been on a break long enough and was ready to get back into advertising.

More recently, I had two Big Jobs in a row that flamed out miserably in two wholly different ways. For both, I'd convinced myself both these jobs were going to be the centerpiece of my career. I'd been so excited for both these jobs, and for them to go so wrong had me really questioning my values and my judgment. So I took a break. I freelanced as a Content Designer for the first time in my career. I took two part-time roles to suss it out, compare and contrast, and see what I responded to.

In that time, my values shifted: away from my sense of self being defined by my title and instead towards work being, well, just work. I was happy enough to use my skills to get money and pay my bills. The healthy detachment stayed with me, even as I decided to pursue and accept a full-time role at one of those companies.

Without these two unexpected breaks, I wouldn't have had the chance to learn some really important things about myself: I'm happiest when I'm doing some sort of writing and that having a Big Title isn't as important as I thought it was. Growth!

Be open to the process

Whenever I find myself in a job-seeking space, I tend to go broad. Even if I have a dream goal in mind ("ooh, I'd love to head up Content Design at the SPCA. Is that a thing?"), I might say yes to any and every conversation, even if it's unlikely that a job will come out of it. This might look like chatting with a friend in a related field, pursuing an informational interview with a place that didn't have any head-count open, or interviewing somewhere that seems like an odd fit.

In having these conversations, I'm learning about the possibilities that are out there, fields I didn't know about, and opportunities I may not have ever considered. More importantly, I'm making connections with new people. I'm learning about them and what they do, and hopefully they're learning a bit about me too.

When you're starting your job hunt, you can be laser-focused on one goal, one path, and one outcome. If you're a little open through the process, you may be able to expand your view, get new perspectives on your own career path, and make some valuable connections along the way.

Let's talk about money

Money matters, obviously. Beyond just how you pay for where you live and keep food coming your way, money in the bank means peace-of-mind. And, America being America, more seems to always mean better. But, what if you became curious about that last bit? What might "enough" look like, and does it all need to come from one place? How can you, as a Designer, use your skills to sufficiently support your life, while not compromising your core values? And do you need to rely on your day-to-day job to feel fulfilled, or can you just earn enough putting your skills to work, while finding creative or other satisfaction elsewhere?

How much is enough?
A good friend of mine, Suz, took a big leap halfway through her career. She'd been working as a Designer in the corporate space for well over a decade, but it was the doodles in the margins of her notebooks that kept drawing her attention. She turned it into real art, and turned that art into a career. At the same time, despite the commissions for murals and regular sale of her pieces, she still needed other work to pay the bills. She spends a few days a week doing some boring-to-her work: overseeing clothing shoots for a big retail client. But it allows her to do what she really loves: make art.

I had a similar, but different experience moving between full-time and freelance. I was saving less and spending more, primarily on boring things like health and dental insurance. And even though the money wasn't likely to work out long-term, it was worth it to me for the experience I gained and what I learned about myself and my relationship to work (and money). I recognize this entire experience is rife with privilege, and I acknowledge that. I have savings, no kids, and a partner with a stable job.

That said, I did get a new perspective on what "enough" meant. My values shifted away from anchoring on "more = better," and instead I understood that enough is ok. What this means now is that I'm less inclined to pursue a promotion for the money reason alone. I don't really want to take on more. I'm satisfied with my current work, and I have time, energy (and money) to balance my life with other things.

So I encourage you to consider: what does enough look like for you?

Can you earn a little less salary and do a little side hustle?
Maybe we set aside the term "side hustle." It feels like you're getting away with something, being sneaky. Maybe instead we find a new way to talk about making money outside your job. And this can be at

any stage in your career: maybe it looks like an Etsy shop where you sell your awesome ceramics. Maybe you set up an ecommerce site where you sell crafts inspired by your love of Australian Shepherds. Maybe you develop and run workshops about storytelling and team-building (Hi, it's me. Please ask me about workshops!).

We're not talking about moonlighting, or doing two jobs at once. That is very likely against your employment agreement. But more about finding ways to have your hobbies or totally not-design-related interests generate some income.

There are tons of ways to supplement your income that are unlikely to violate your employment agreement (this is not legal advice. Please consult a lawyer if you have any real questions). But you can often do these things without being sneaky about it. Talk to your manager or HR person. It's likely totally fine as long as it doesn't take away from your working hours or leverage any proprietary information or property (please see a lawyer for reals).

On the other hand, taking what you love and turning it into a money-making endeavor can be a quick way to zap the fun out of it. That's doubly true if you're relying on the income to make ends meet. You might find yourself crunched for time, or having trouble switching gears from your job to your side hustle. There's good and bad to it, so go in with your eyes wide open.

Can you gain experience that pays off later?
Another way to frame your income is by viewing it as experience. Yes, I realize you can't pay your utilities with vibes, but maybe you can do some short-term belt-tightening in order to have medium or long-term gains. This might look like taking a more junior position in a different domain (like going from a social media company to fintech if that's what you think you're more into). It could also look like

shifting roles entirely. I've seen very senior Content Designers shift to becoming more junior Product Designers, because they wanted to take their career path in a different way. I've taken a cut in hours in order to teach a semester at a local college, just for the experience and the exposure. There are all different ways and reasons to design your career in a non-traditional way. Keep an open mind.

Lou Adler, an incredibly respected voice in the area of recruitment and hiring, anchors a lot of his advice on the concept of a "career move." And it isn't all about money:

> "A true career move [is] not an ill-defined lateral transfer with a bit more money. In my mind, a true career move involves a 30% non-monetary increase. In this case, the 30% is a combination of job stretch (a bigger job), increased job satisfaction (doing more satisfying work with more impact) and job growth (being in a situation that offers more upside potential). While compensation is not unimportant, it should not be the most important reason a person accepts your offer."
> – Lou Adler, CEO and founder of Performance-based Hiring and Learning Systems

Your career path is yours to create. There isn't one right way to do it, and I'll invite you to reject the framing of "traditional" and "non-traditional." Take a detour, learn a new skill, mix it up. As long as you're aligned with your values and working to your strengths, the only person you need to answer to is you.

Takeaways

Define your values to set a path
Understand what you value: skills growth, life balance, ethics, wealth,

etc. and use your values to consider the next steps in your career.

Look back to look forward

Reflect on your past experience to inform where you want to go next. What worked, what didn't, and why?

Expand your mind

Consider steps in your career that are outside your mental model of options: freelancing, consulting, or taking a new path altogether.

CHAPTER TWO

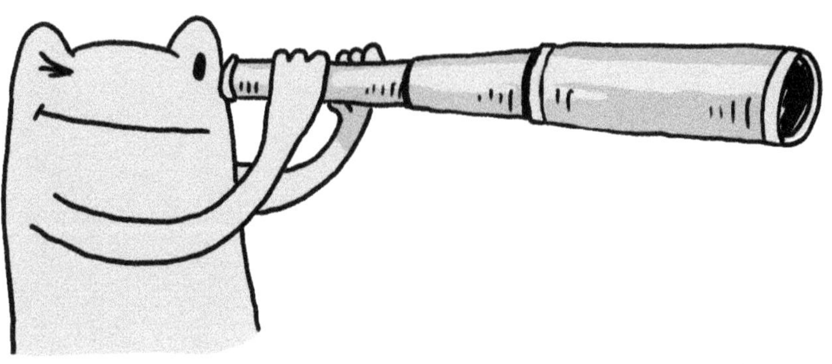

Setting up your search

Like undertaking a massive cooking effort, setting up a job search takes preparation. You can't just put a pot on the stove, fire up the burner, and hope you have everything you need. Setting up a job search means taking a bit of inventory, making a few useful lists, and then going about things in a logical order. Ready? Hungry? Let's get to work.

Start with self-reflection

Why are you here? What are you looking for? What is the point? What is the meaning of life? Why even work?

Ok, ok, we may have gone too existential, too quickly there. But starting with some healthy self-reflection before you start trawling LinkedIn is probably a good idea. No matter if you're starting a job

search of your own volition (quietly unhappy, anticipating layoffs, looking for a new challenge) or not (new grad, a recent severance agreement, the layoff fairy finally visited you), begin by asking yourself some key questions:

- What is it in your work that you really love doing, where the time goes away and you're in the zone?
- What is some work you've done in the past that you are really proud of, and why? What aspect about it was most exciting? The domain, the outcome, who you worked with?
- Do you have strong feelings about being a manager or being an individual contributor (IC)?

Starting to dig into what's worked (and not worked) in your past experience will help you start developing your must-haves and nice-to-haves list for your next role. When you start looking, you're going to be met with a whole lot of variables, and because you might be excited or anxious or desperate, you might be pretty quick to compromise. Job searching is an emotional enterprise, so keeping your effort as honest and fact-forward as possible can keep you focused, grounded, and hopefully, have you landing somewhere that's truly a good fit.

Make a list (an actual list) that starts to detail out the things that you're looking for in your next role. Go big and go exhaustive. Think about what you'd ideally be doing, who'd you be working with, what collaboration looks like.

This might include:

- Core skills of your role you love doing
- Certain domains you're passionate or are super curious about
- Do you want to work at a small, medium, or big company? Why?
- Maturity of org: do you want to be the founding designer or do

you want to join an established team?
- Manager or IC?
- Lots of collaboration or lone wolf?
- Establish 0 to 1 operational practices (e.g., critique, XFN collab) or inherit existing ones?

For now, let's hold off considering title, salary requirements, or seniority. Think less about what the next entry on your resume is, and more about the job itself. How do you want to spend your time? What's exciting and motivating to you personally? And don't think that your answer is obvious. You might think "Doesn't everyone want to be a Senior Design Manager working on the cutting edge of AI at a start-up?" My god, no. To some, that's their own idea of hell. It's more than ok if you *just* want to be a Designer, working on something interesting (enough) at a mid-size company. Now, go on and generate a list!

Get serious about logistics

Beyond what you're working on, where you're going to be working is a good thing to keep in mind before you start your search.

In-person, remote, and everything in between
Since the pandemic started, work has gotten a lot more flexible (until it seemed to revert back a bit). Still, the options are out there and knowing what works best for you is a big factor into your job search. Fully remote? In-person every day? Hybrid? Flexible? Where you'll be doing your job might be just as important as the job itself. Consider what works best for you, what you're willing to compromise on, and how you'll decide. Do you need in-person collaboration to feel connected to the work and your co-workers? Do you have logistical or personal considerations why you'd do your best work at home? Are you open to anything?

Relo or no

In my early 20s, I was just starting out as a copywriter, and didn't have anything tying me to where I was. My search was broad and my options were open. I scattered my portfolio up and down the West Coast and ended up landing a job at Wieden + Kennedy (I honestly still don't know how that happened). I was young, I was flexible, I was excited to take the leap to Portland.

Now? It's another story. I've been living in San Francisco coming up on two decades (I honestly still don't know how that happened either). I have a husband with a law practice based in California. We have a mortgage. I ain't going anywhere for any job. This might limit my opportunities in the future, but it's something I know I can't compromise on. And to be honest, after seeing the volatility of the market since the pandemic, picking up and moving a life isn't like a bet we're willing to take. Ask me about my friend who left SF after 20 years to relocate his family to the other side of the world, only to see the position be eliminated after 90 days. Oof.

Should you stay at the same company or should you go?

This goes out to all the people who are currently employed, but considering looking elsewhere. Back when the job market was hot (and even when it wasn't), I know I was quite quick to move on from a suboptimal situation. Getting a new job seemed easier than trying to fix a given problem, and because I enjoyed interviewing (hence why I'm the weirdo writing this book), I didn't hesitate putting myself out there.

Looking back, I think I could have done a little more to stay at some of the places I left. I think I thought I was stuck, when really I could have done a little more work to remove some obstacles like a weird manager relationship or a seemingly untenable commute. That said, when

I was at a truly toxic workplace or one where my values were in full misalignment, moving on was the right move.

So before you really start looking, maybe consider your ways to stay.

Going somewhere else in the company

Maybe you've been stuck on one team for a little too long, or you're no longer doing work that's interesting to you. Maybe there's something new spinning up in another department or some old work that no one's been prioritizing. Look around, do some informational interviews with people you know and trust and see where the conversations take you. You don't have to frame it like "I'm moving teams or else," more like "I'm interested in finding out more about you, your team, and what you're working on."

Getting transferred to another office

If you work at a company with multiple locations and relocation is on the table for you, then consider poking around and learning what's happening in the other offices. Maybe a change of scenery, a change in the way you work, in what you see every day might be sufficient for you to feel into the work again. Not all companies will pay you to relocate, but it might be worth it to you if you get to keep your same job (and equity, if it's relevant), even if that means a self-move somewhere new.

Finding a different role in the company

Even if you've been a Designer for awhile, it's never too late for a career change. Content Design is my second career after I spent a decade in advertising. I've seen Content Designers become PMs, Engineers become Program Managers, and Marketers, um, ok they just usually stay Marketers. The point being, if there's a discipline you want to learn more about, start talking to them. See if there's a rotational program or another way to start doing that thing. You

might be able to make a transformation, right in the very office you're already badging into.

Moving from an IC to a Manager (or the other way)

For a long time, the only way to progress in design was to go from a junior to a mid-level to senior, to manager, to director. The path was well-trodden, the path was expected. But here's the thing: managing and designing are two totally different skillsets. And not everyone is good at both (ask me how many times I've learned this lesson. It is many times). Just because you love designing doesn't mean you'll love managing. Now, there are many more people going straight up the IC path, even getting to a director or VP title. No managing, no reports. If you feel like you're stuck as a Manager, or feel fomo when your designers are showing work, maybe see how it feels to take on some IC work. If you're an IC, consider seeing how you can work mentoring or managing into your scope. This might look like advising junior designers or taking on an intern for the summer. Like a pet! (Interns are not pets. Pay your interns.)

Your job search strategy (how to not make your job search a full-time job)

When you start looking for a job, it can begin to take over your life. The LinkedIn algorithm machine will start working for (and against) you. Once it starts picking up signals that you're looking, you'll start to get served open positions (often with less and less relevancy), thirsty asks to set up job search alerts, and notifications will start multiplying like tribbles (look it up, non-nerds). You are in charge of your search, not the machines. Here's how to protect your time and not let it get away from you.

Get real about your timeline

- If you have a job and you think layoffs are coming, maybe plan around that. Don't worry about the market getting saturated or searching out of fear.
- If you are without a job, consider freelancing or doing something else entirely while you find your forever home. This might look like project work, or relevant to what you want to do, but not exactly what you do type work.
- If you're on funemployment or have a severance, factor that in.

Set boundaries and stick to them

Set aside an hour, maybe two for job-search related activities per day. Maybe even less than that. You don't need to constantly be trolling for new positions and you don't need to be the first (or even first 100) to apply. And please ignore "over 1000 applications have been received" on LinkedIn. So many of those are people that are going scatter-shot in their approach. Don't be that person.

Don't be scattershot in your approach

Think of every job application as a fishing line. Every time you send one out, you now have to manage, think about, and monitor that fishing line. Even if it's a longshot, you're still tracking it in the back of your mind. It's not healthy. Plus, the more you apply to jobs you're not really right for, or you don't really want, the more rejections you're likely to get. And even if you didn't want the role in the first place, those emails still sting, even just a little.

Make a damn spreadsheet

You can't keep it all in your head. Make a spreadsheet that lists out the roles you've applied to, the last time you took action, and your current status with that role. Link back to the job description, your recruiter and other contacts, and make time every week to update the spreadsheet. Thank me later.

Don't go it alone: psychological safety and the job search

Job searching is not easy. It's not rewarding (until it is) and it's a lot of work for one good payoff. And there's emotional toil too: you're putting yourself out there with every application, every cover letter, every conversation. You're vulnerable, waiting to be judged, and that's exactly what's happening. Day in, day out. That's a lot to do by yourself. So here are some ways to take care of yourself.

Don't start until you're ready

> "One mistake I made in past job searches was taking the first job that was offered when I was ready to leave. I didn't do as much research as I should have. I was burned out and was just ready for something new and different."
> – Taylor Howard, Principal Content Designer, Cash App

If you just got let go from a job, or if you're in a really tough place in your current job and dealing with a whole lot of difficult times, it's not the right time to be putting yourself out there to look for a job. The best approach to getting a role is to come at it from a place of genuine curiosity and excitement. Not feigned, not trying to make an impression. Real interest. You're not going to have the capacity to develop that perspective if you're still reeling from a layoff or trudging through a really shitty situation. Don't get going out of desperation. Take some time to get prepared, to do some research. To really get in mind what it is you want before you start applying everywhere and anywhere out of fear.

Find a friend

When I found myself on the job hunt a few years ago, it was right around the time that layoffs were just beginning to hit the industry. There was a lot of chatter on various Slacks about job hunting and

what roles were open and where. I connected with a couple of former colleagues who were also looking, and we stayed in regular touch with each other: commiserating, connecting one another with jobs we came across, and providing advice and referrals as needed. Even though sometimes we were applying for the same job, it didn't feel competitive, but collaborative. While we kept it casual, you can also set some rigor with your job search buddy: how often you meet, how much info you want to share, if you want to practice your presentations and pitches. Tap your network to find a buddy, or simply connect with a current or former colleague. If they're not looking, maybe they know someone who is.

> "It helps to have a peer group of people to collaborate with who are rooting for you. Sometimes I just need a few minutes of cheerleading. It was so useful, especially when you're interviewing alone, in your house."
> – Margie Levinson, Content Design Manager, Warner Music

Margie also told me about *Never Search Alone*, a job-searching approach by Phyl Terry. Beyond the book, there are also great resources for job-search councils, where you can get connected with a peer group for support and accountability.

Take a break (every day, and maybe longer)

Job searching is a lot. It's easy to get obsessive, to let it spiral. And if you're not having any luck, give yourself the grace to take a break. The break doesn't have to be long: honestly, just an hour away to go stare at the ocean or hike up a mountain can be a bit of a reset (don't look at your phone. Don't do it. Leave it.) But even a day or two of not taking any *new* action by you can be a good break. You want to be ready, psychologically and in all the other ways when you're job searching. Keep an eye on yourself and tap out when you need to.

Takeaways

Let your past inform your future

The reason you're seeking a new job might inform the kind of job you're looking for. Before you start hitting the job postings, think carefully about where you've been successful and happy.

Write it down

Start making a list of your strengths, skills, core requirements and interests. Stack-rank them and keep the list close.

Do the self-care thing

A job search can be really taxing. Make sure you're in the right headspace to get into it and take a break (even if it's just for an afternoon).

CHAPTER THREE

Artifacts of a search: resumes, case studies, and sites

From resumes to case studies, entire portfolios to personal web sites, the artifacts of a job search serves to tell the story of you. Each element comes together to tell a consistent, cohesive story focusing on your strengths, your skills, and what the next chapter in your career looks like.

Really good resumes

Oh, resumes. CVs. Despite LinkedIn telling any recruiter all the information they would really need to know about a candidate, resumes

are still hanging around as a must-have. They haven't really evolved much, and they do serve a useful function: give an at-a-glance look to what a given candidate is all about. And there's a catch-22 built into resumes: they have to be detailed, they have to be perfect, and, most likely, they're only going to be scanned or glanced at. So structure matters. Design matters. And details matter (even if they're barely read).

Structure first

If you're lucky, a human being will be scanning your resume. But, with the robots taking over, your resume is very likely to be scanned by some sort of machine called ATS or Applicant Tracking Software. The cool thing is that the same way you'd want to optimize your resume for humans is the same way you'd want to optimize your resume for machines: simple, straightforward structure. There's nothing wrong with using a template, and there are a million templates out there. Resumes are not the place to get creative. Create clear sections, use bullet points, keep it short, keep it scannable.

Tell your story in facts

Even though resumes are boring, they still tell a story. Your story. Where you went to school and what you studied, how that led you to a first job, how your career has evolved, what you've focused on. Resumes should follow a structure that ladders up to the job you're applying for, the one that focuses on your strengths, your skills, and what you want to do next in your career.

Don't pad your damn resume

Avoid the fluff, avoid the filler, and don't pad your resume. Be honest, take credit where it's due, but don't go over the top. Recruiters and hiring managers can read through the tone and filler of a padded resume: they've seen it all before and they'll be too quick to dismiss you. Every experience you have had is relevant experience. Being a barista

probably taught you how to move fast under high pressure situations. Being an intern at your local newspaper probably taught you how to be resourceful and the importance of fact-checking. You don't need to say that you were a "coffee creator" or an "entry-level editorial lead."

Telling the story of your work with case studies

Case studies are a storytelling exercise: what's the context, what is the final scene. They're usually presentations or presentation-like objects that explain the how/why/and why-should-I-care of any given project you've worked on. You might have a case study that shows off a feature you built, a student project you completed, or a process or system you created. Case studies give narrative and context to the screenshots and design file artifacts of what we do.

> "You are the product of your case studies."
> -Leslie Forman

Well lucky you, you're already ahead of the game, because I know you've been keeping track of your work and writing case studies as soon as the project shipped, right? Right? Oh...right. Well, now is as good a time as any to get started!

While case studies showcase the product, the company, and the outcome of any given project, the true story that case studies show is the story of you: what your strengths are, what you're interested in, the work you're most proud of. From end to end, every case study should reinforce what you're about. This doesn't mean showing off, taking credit where it isn't due, or making "I" the most prominent word in the study. It means continuing to highlight the skills you have, the work you love, and help hiring managers picture where you'd be most successful in their team.

How to choose what to do a study on

> "I'm looking for portfolios that show a balance of process, craft, and a clear understanding of the user and the business. Start by creating a portfolio website and 3–4 case studies of the work you want to be hired to do. Specifically, if you want to be hired as a product designer, then there's no need to share brand or print work unless your product design case studies don't show strong visual design."
> –Leslie Yang, "What a Hiring Manager Looks for in Product Design Portfolios and Presentations"

A friend of mine had been working at the same place for six years. Most of his time he'd spent on a product he loved, but due to some reorgs, he'd been stuck doing work he wasn't as interested in the last year or so. In putting his case studies together, he started to draw on the most recent work because it felt more relevant and had some good metrics to show for it.

"Did you like doing that work?" I asked him.

"Not particularly," he said. "It was easy, but boring. But it shipped!"

"Is this the kind of work you want to do in the future?" I pressed.

"Yeah, no," he admitted.

"Then don't make a case study out of it."

Telling the story of your work is telling the story of you: what you're interested in, what your skills and strengths are, and what you'd like to work on. When a hiring panel is listening to your case studies, they're starting to imagine how to take your past experience and

apply it to the problems they're trying to solve. Choosing your case study is functionally writing your own ticket: this is what I do, this is what I'm about, this is the thing you should hire me for.

I have a case study in my book that's from 2020, and I think it's unlikely I'll take it out anytime soon. It's work I'm proud of, that I really enjoyed doing. It was about integrity, solving a really tricky ethics problem at scale, had a ton of great collaboration, and was about a topic I cared about: misinformation about health and civics. Even though I haven't worked at that company in a long time and the work itself may not even be live anymore, the story I tell there is about my interests, my impact, and the kind of work that I love to do. It's a keeper.

Building a variable case study bank

Not all case studies are the same: some are big centerpieces that tell the story of a year-long project. Some are medium size ones that highlight a particular interaction, domain knowledge or lesson. Some are little bite-size guys that maybe don't stand on their own, but might serve as a small lesson, insight or skill to show.

- Centerpiece study
  This is the one that goes into every review, that's the center of your portfolio. You'll have a few different versions of it to scale to presentation mode: passive on your site, as a leave-behind, and as a live presentation. It shows end-to-end thinking, a variety of skills, and basically says "this is exactly the kind of work I want to do in the future"

  Ex: an entire app you designed or redesigned, a complex feature, a single feature with multiple iterations or launches

- Medium study

  These stories, while still important, don't take up as much oxygen as your big centerpiece story. These case studies might highlight 2-3 key points; acquisition of domain knowledge, a particular insight or lesson, or a way in which you made an impact as a result of this work. Maybe you navigated a perceived failure, or there was a community you were able to directly impact. These are great to show a different angle or way of working that might not be present in your centerpiece story.

  Ex: a naming exercise, designing prototypes for a research study, a smaller feature, a settings redesign

- Bite-sized study

  These are little examples of work, of interpersonal interactions, of small things you did that might not warrant an entire case study, but still show a singular skill or idea. They may just be one or two screens, or highlight a single line of text.

  Ex: something you did in office hours that made a big difference, a quick rewrite that built trust and relationships

Structuring case studies

Before you even get started outlining and writing your case study, think about what skill or strength it is you want to place front and center. That might look like: collaboration with cross-functional people, a specific design skill like prototyping or naming, working in a specific domain like health or finance, or thinking strategically under tight timelines. Choose one or two skills to highlight, and that will determine what you include (and what can be left out).

If you've heard of the "STAR" format of interview question, the same acronym will serve you here (and if STAR is new to you, we'll get into it as we interview-prep in Chapter 5).

STAR is:
Situation / Task / Action / Result

In interviewing, it means answering questions by telling a structured story that gives just enough context to show the kind of work you did and why it mattered. You can take the same approach in designing your case study. Note: not all sections are created equal. You want to spend a lot more time on what you actually did than on the set-up or the outcome.

Situation (10% of your case study): What was the context of this work? This might include a bit about the company (if it's not a widely known one), a little bit about the team (if it's important), and any other context that sets up how you did whatever you did to solve a problem.

Task (10% of your case study): Simply put: what was the problem you were aiming to solve. What were you tasked with? This might look like a business or a user problem (or, as it is in most cases, both!)

Action (70% of your case study): Ah, welcome to the main event! Now you get to get into what you did and how you did it. You might talk about how you approached the problem, the research you did, relationships you built, the unexpected things that happened along the way, and the triumph of your accomplishment at the end. This is when you are the hero of your story, where, as we quoted Leslie Forman in the opening: the product of your case study is you. Don't be shy: this is your big chance to highlight the kind of work that means something to you, the way you work best, and the kind of work that you'd want to do again.

Result (10% of your study): Nu, what happened? What did all the work result in? Beyond those metrics you grabbed from your PM at the end of the project, what else did this mean? Better relationships between you and a troubled department? Did it set up further work in the future? Get you rehired in a contract gig? Show those bullet points of impact! Line 'em up!

Actually making the thing

Now that you have the work you're going to highlight and the rough structure of the story, how do you go about actually making the thing? Well, that depends on what your plan is for your case study: where it's going to live, how the story is going to be told, etc. Are you putting it up on a web site? Sending it along as an attachment? Presenting it in an interview? It's likely in the course of a job search, you'll need to take your case study and scale it up/scale it back depending on context. Consider making a few versions: one that can stand on its own without you voicing over and filling in the gaps, and one that's a presentation that needs you there to make sense.

Article-style

Written like a blog post, the article-like form tells the story from end to end. Inset visuals support the story as you tell it, highlighting key moments, screens, or take-aways.

The presentation

This is the version you'd prepare for an on-site interview or case study presentation. More visually focused, you want to have fewer words on the screen because you'll be telling the story live and in person.

The presentation (annotated)

Like the in-person presentation, your annotated version might

function as a leave-behind, or something that lives on your website. Still visually centered, add in coherent notes or captions to tell the story behind what the viewer sees.

So you want to build a web site

Personal web sites are still a thing, and probably a useful investment of your time and money. They don't have to be super complex or totally detailed. But they're a great place to craft your story, highlight the things about you that you want to tell, and hold all your damn work. Core sections might include:

- **About me**
  Just a little synopsis of who you are and what you do: the job you'd like (or the job you have), your villain origin story, or your hopes and dreams.

- **Case studies**
  Have them live here and you can link to them as needed. You can organize them however you'd like: by specialty, by company, by focus, or something else.

- **Resume**
  Nice to have a link to the damn thing. People like them!

- **Everything else**
  Have a relevant hobby you want to showcase? Videos of presentations you've done? Cool animation studies you wouldn't mind showing off? Here's where they live.

Don't go it alone

Hey, over-achiever. Can you do it all? Yes. Should you? Maybe not. Is this the time to learn how to code or write or design? Maybe not. Lean on your friends, or, if you can, hire experts. While my strength is in writing, I know I can always use design help. When I was putting together my site, I paid a friend to skillfully build it on Squarespace. While I absolutely could have spent time learning the tool and doing it myself, I knew they could do it better and faster. What's more, they have a keen design eye, and would have tended to the little details I might not notice. This means that my site may not be dismissed from more design-focused visitors then those just coming for the hot content takes.

If you're a writer, find a designer (and vice versa).

If you can't build it, find a friend.

Other people make your work better. This is one of those times.

Takeaways

Build a story into your resume
Resumes are a structured narrative. The next chapter should be the job you're applying for.

Ask for what you want
Lead with the work you want to do again, not what you think impresses people.

No lies, no exaggerations
Be honest. Padding and fluffing only gets you in hot water.

CHAPTER FOUR

Reading job listings and reaching recruiters

> "It's like dating; if it's good you know right away, if it's bad, you know right away. And you only need one job at a time."
> -Leslie Forman

Dating, my mother told me, is a numbers game. You have to meet a lot of people and go on a lot of dates to find the right match. This advice may have been true before the advent of online dating, where you can filter out things that are deal-breakers for you (like smokers, people who like the band Eagles, or those who make going to Burning Man their entire identity). And dating is exhausting. Emotionally,

physically, and it takes up too much time. Why waste time making plans, getting ready, getting your hopes up if it isn't going to go anywhere?

Same with searching for a job.

Job searching is more than just a time commitment. It's an emotional commitment as well. Every time you hit "apply" on a posting, you're planting a small seed of hope. And the more you apply, the more little bits of hope you have. And that alone is fine. But every rejection, no matter how inevitable, stings. And those little cuts can dig into your self-confidence, your conviction, and your overall resilience.

Job searching is not a numbers game. It is about being practical, being tactical, and knowing when you have the capacity and ability to be fully present. So, how do you go about choosing when to click "apply" and when to let it go.

It starts with reading job listings.

Job listings: search and destroy

As you fire up the LinkedIn machine to get your search going, keep your list of must-haves and nice-to-haves handy. They will guide you in deciding what looks good, what makes you want to learn more, and what makes you say, "Thank you, next."

Job titles are a minefield

Content Designer, Content Strategist, Content Specialist, UX Writer: are these all the same job? Sometimes, but not always! Titles are not consistent across the industry, and not just for content folks. Your job search is not a time to get hung up on titles. Think of them as just

search terms, not a measure or summary of what the job really is. Start with a broad search "content" or "design," then get into the details to see what the job is really about.

Believe the details

Once you've moved past the title, start to look closely at the job description, in particular the area of focus, the domain, and the bullet points. Anything that doesn't feel boilerplate in a job description was a choice made by the hiring manager or person in charge of this role. That means you should believe them. Look here for your strengths, skills, tools, or anything else that's specific to you and your interest in this job. Also keep an eye out for red flags or things that turn you off. Don't like ecommerce or B2B? Then don't apply for a job that mentions that as a key differentiator.

Don't get dazzled by perks, pay, and perceptions

Job descriptions are sales pitches. They are trying to entreat the perfect candidate to apply, and are not only beckoning them with the explanation of the job details, but all the company has to offer. And they may sound great (Daily cupcakes for you and your family! Free pony rides! Trips to the actual moon!), but make sure you're focusing on the core aspects of the job. You're looking for a job that fits you, plays to your strengths, and matches your criteria. And take those huge pay postings with a grain of salt: they are likely to include stock grants based on today's valuation over a four-year vesting schedule. Anything can happen with "maybe money" like that.

In the end, be selective about which jobs you apply for. You really want to treat each one like something you're willing to see through, all the way to an offer and then doing the actual job. Each one is a little emotional investment, even if all you're doing is a one-click quick apply. That said, each job description doesn't have to be perfect. If you come across one that's a "maybe," then consider applying so you

potentially have the opportunity to have your questions answered. Be realistic, but keep an open mind at the same time. You never know what you might find or the people you might meet.

Cover letters (ugh)

I am functionally a writer by trade. Writing comes pretty easily to me, and I don't take that for granted. I am also still a human being who hates writing cover letters. They are the worst. But, as a hiring manager, they can really make a candidate stand out. The good news is, if you apply a little Content Design skill, you only need to be faced with that terrible blank page once.

Make yourself a little template

There are about a trillion cover letter examples on the internet. Start there, and see what you like. It is totally ok to adapt existing templates for structure, for style, for formatting. Find something you like, and make a little outline. That might look like:

- a boilerplate intro that explains who you are and what you're interested in
- a list of supporting bullet points that detail your strengths and relevant experience
- a boilerplate sign-off

The things that will change, based on the role, are those bullet points. Make them relevant to the job post, make them specific to your strengths, and make the whole thing punchy.

Make it personalized

While you're working with a template, you also want to make it specific to the job and why you're interested in it. For example, when I

was applying for the role at Peloton, I said,

> "It's not just because I'm a Peloton fan (celebrating 500 rides this Sunday with Christine), or because I'm looking for a new opportunity. It's because since I joined Peloton, I've seen so many opportunities for Content Design to make a difference in the product."

I did my best to tie in my love of the product with my expertise as a Content Designer, and in the end, it worked.

Keep it short, keep it scannable

You don't want to write a long cover letter, and the recruiter doesn't want to read one. Keep things short and honest, to the point and totally personalized. Don't add fluff or filler, and this isn't the time to detail all your accomplishments since graduating high school. And make it about the company. This isn't about why this is a perfect job for you, personally. Or what it would mean to you. It's about explaining why your experience, strengths and skills make you the person who will bring the most to the company, to the position, to the organization as a whole. This is where your sales job begins (the one where you are the product).

Work your network

Once you've found a job you're interested in, and you've got your cover letter and resume all ready for the application, don't apply. What? Right. While you may end up clicking the link in the form to submit it all, take a minute first to tap your network and see if there's another way in. A little help from someone on the inside might be the help you need.

Use LinkedIn as intended

On LinkedIn, see if you know anyone who works at the company. No matter how tenuous the connection might be, it still might be a good foot in the door. Many companies offer referral bonuses for existing employees to recommend candidates. So even if your connection is someone you met briefly at a conference or meet-up, or a former co-worker from the pizza place in college, any connection will do.

Search for mutuals

If you can sort it out, maybe figure out who the hiring manager might be, or someone else who works in that department. Say you're applying for a "Design" position in "Growth" at "Salesforce," use those search terms to find someone who is working in Design in Growth at Salesforce. Maybe you find a few hits. Maybe you have someone in common with those people. Ask your person in common to see if they'd be open to introduce you, or maybe find out more about what it's like to work in Design in Growth at Salesforce. Nothing to lose, everything to gain.

If all else fails, then just apply for the job

Even if you're still building your network, if you're a recent grad, or if you're doing a bit of a career change, it's still worth applying for that job. Those connections might make a difference, or it might mean nothing at all. Oh, and if you apply for that job and then find out you have a connection, you haven't missed the boat. You can still hit up that person to ask the hiring manager to keep an eye out for your application. Never too late!

The emotional toll of looking for a job in design

While all parts of the job application process can be at once exciting and defeating, the early stages of trying to get bites on your applications are particularly fraught. Apply, wait, repeat. You might get immediate

rejections from jobs you thought were a sure thing. You might get an initial response, then nothing for a long time. You might hear nothing at all. When you start to get down, there are ways to take care of yourself.

Take a break

Job searching can be all-consuming, and can absolutely become a full-time job. One that has shitty benefits and no pay. If you can, even if it's just for an afternoon, take time away from the search screen. You don't need to be the first one to apply, even if another perfect job comes through the search results while you're away.

Turn to your network

Not to find a job, but to find support. If you're not already in one, ask your former coworkers or classmates if there's a Slack you can be a part of. Those clustered communities can be hard to find, but can be invaluable for getting reassurance, especially in a job search.

Go to the archives

If you find yourself facing rejection over and over, which happens a ton in a job search, it can start to feel personal. And it's hard to remember that, for most of the time, it isn't. Before you end up in the spiraling tank of a desolation pit, know what it'll take to get you out of it. Therapy is great! Also, keep copies of your old reviews, peer feedback, or even check out any LinkedIn endorsements. Believe the good things people have said about you (and don't believe the negative self-talk chatter that's cluttering your head).

Takeaways

Job listings are all about the details

Dig deep to find the facts about the job, the company, and what you need to have to be successful there.

Templatize your cover letter

Make it true to you, customized to the company and the role, and adaptable through your job search.

Job searching is emotionally taxing

Each application is a little exercise in hope, and rejections can be compounding in their impact. Apply selectively, and take a break when you need to.

CHAPTER FIVE

Everything before the interview

Once you've gotten a bite on an application or connected with a recruiter, you'll start getting into the gauntlet of interviews. Some will be surprisingly simple screens and others will be more formal portfolio presentations. No matter what kind of interview you've got lined up, you'll want to prepare to tell the story of you.

So much of interviewing is about storytelling: you are telling your story about how you came to be a Designer, the story of your career, and all the stories that make up your experience. The more you can prepare these stories and get them ready to answer the questions that

come your way, the better you'll feel in an interview.

The story of you isn't one-size-fits-all. It's going to flex depending on who you're talking to, the company you're applying to, and the questions you're asked. You might want to highlight one area of experience over another, a particular strength or skill you have, or an interest outside of work that's relevant to the job.

Telling your story for a recruiter

Congrats! Your resume (and maybe cover letter) have broken through, and you're on your way to chatting with a recruiter. The role of the recruiter can differ, depending on if they are an internal or external recruiter. An internal recruiter works directly for the company, and may have more insight into the team, the company culture, and the work you'll be doing. An external recruiter often works for a staffing agency, and their motivations might be more about getting the job filled by any means necessary, rather than making sure it's exactly the right person for the job.

> "Recruiting, in its purest and most successful expression, is about building symbiotic relationships. It creates the conditions that support a successful match between candidate and context, and between work and meaning."
> –Josh Silverman, Founder & CEO, PeopleWork Partners

In both cases, recruiters want to quickly suss out if you're a viable candidate. This looks like making sure you are who you say you are, the story you tell them aligns with the story they interpreted from your resume, and that all the logistical pieces work. Those logistics are things like where the company is located, in-office expectations, and salary expectations.

Telling your (short) story for a recruiter

Your goal in this conversation is to tell your story efficiently and help the recruiter conclude, "yes, this candidate has the baseline things we're looking for." If you're lucky, they'll start with a little ramble about the job, the company, or any specifics about the position. Listen closely and read between the lines. The details you hear are what you can reflect back in your own story, not just in this conversation, but for the rest of the interview process.

Next up, they'll likely have a pretty open prompt with something like "Tell me a bit about yourself."

You'll want to hit three key beats:

1. A little relevant context on your background
2. Why you're looking for a job right now
3. Why this job is a match to your background, strengths, and values

Say you were a new grad, and then got hired at a big tech company to work on Accessibility. You were there for a few years but then you got laid off. It's something you're an expert on, are passionate about, and want to continue working on. An Accessibility job is posted at a medium-size outdoors ecommerce company and you apply.

Your "tell me a bit about yourself" might sound like:
"After getting my Masters in UX Design at California College of the Arts, I landed a great role at Adobe working on Accessibility. I got to work with teams all over the company, and shipped products that made a difference. When I got laid off, I knew I wanted to take everything I've learned about Accessibility and continue with it in my next role. When I'm not improving interactive experiences for people with disabilities, I love to be outside: I rock climb, hike and kayak. When I saw your job posted, I couldn't wait to apply. I'd be thrilled to bring my Accessibility skills to an industry I really care about."

It really can be that short and sweet. You can certainly pepper in a few more details, grabbing some of those crucial points you heard in the recruiter's preamble, or read in the job description. Help the recruiter connect the dots with every answer to their questions.

How to get what you need from a recruiter

Just as the recruiter is trying to get some basic information from you, this is also the time to get some key information from them. You can ask them questions that will help inform how you prepare for future interviews, like the strengths or skills this person should have, or learning more about why this role is open. The more you can learn, the better positioned you will be for interviews in the future. Besides, it's crucial that you always have questions to ask in every interview: it demonstrates that you're curious, you're interested, and you're well-prepared.

> "If they're good at their job, recruiters are on your side, they want you to succeed. They're going to be your best collaborators through the process. Ask them about the interview structure, about what kinds of questions you're going to be asked, if there's going to be a section for 'collaboration' or 'craft' or whatever else."
> -Andy Welfle, co-author of *Writing Is Designing*

Questions you might ask include:

- Why is this role open?
- What does the cross-functional team look like?
- What's the ratio of Product Design/Content Design/Research/PM?
- Who does this role report to? Who does that person report to?
- Are there any travel expectations for this role?
- What does the in-office requirement look like?
- Will I have a chance to/be expected to show my portfolio?

The recruiter might not have all the answers. You may want to hold some of your discipline-specific questions for when you talk to the

hiring manager. The recruiter might not know the specific background, strengths, or skills this role requires. You can certainly ask them, but don't be surprised if you get an "I don't know, I'll ask the hiring manager," as a response.

Hopefully, the recruiter will bring up salary requirements in the initial conversation. This means that before either side gets too invested (emotionally, time-wise), no one is disappointed if an offer comes in insultingly low. Uncomfortable speaking about salary? Good news: you don't have to say much. In fact, all you need to say is one short sentence, then stop talking. Don't justify, don't explain. Say the number and STFU.

It goes like this:

"My salary expectation is <$175,000>*" *(or)*

"I'd like to get to <$175,000>*"

*insert your generous, but reasonable expectation here. It doesn't matter what your current salary is, or what the (alleged) going rate is for your role. You will have done your research, calculated what makes it worth it to you, and determined a number.

Again, say the number, and STFU.

Telling your stories for everyone else

Once you're past the recruiter screen, you'll likely be set up with 1:1 interviews, then move to a panel. More 1:1s may come after that. This is where you'll be doing the bulk of your storytelling. To feel comfortable, confident, and natural in telling your stories, there's a bit more work you'll have to do.

Play guess the question

Before you start to think about the answers, do some brainstorming about the questions that might come your way. These might be about your background, why you're interested in this role, or why you're interested in the company. Maybe you have gaps or twists in your resume that have elicited questions before. Maybe making a move to this role would be a twist in and of itself. Brainstorm, research, and write down any and all the questions you can think of that might come your way. Next we'll work on how to answer them.

Create a STAR story bank

STAR (Situation, Task, Action, Result) is a way to structure your experience into repeatable, coherent stories. You give someone just enough context to understand the situation, highlight your role and contribution, then show what the result of your action was. It's the same structure we talked about using for building your case studies, but it comes in handy when answering questions live in an interview as well.

Situation (1-2 sentences). When or where did the event take place? What was the context? Why was this a problem? What was the business need?

Task (1-2 sentences). What was your role in the situation? Why did this come to you? Explain your agency: was this task assigned to you, or did you see the need for this problem to be solved?

Action (3-5 sentences). What did you do: your specific contributions, the steps you took, the decisions you made. What barriers or speedbumps did you hit along the way? How did you overcome them? Focus on what you did, but contextualize it in terms of how you collaborated with a team.

Result (1-2 sentences). What changed as a result of the action you

took? Did you move key metrics? Build relationships? Learn something? Change a behavior or process? Why is this important?

STAR stories aren't custom-made. You can reuse stories to answer more than one question.

Sample story:

At Lyft, I was working as a Content Designer on a very tricky new feature, In-app Audio Recording. There were many sensitive messages to convey, and user research had shown a lot of mistrust and misinterpretations of how the feature worked. The team was brand new, and didn't have a lot of experience working with Content Design. **(Situation)**

Because I knew there were a lot of players with a lot of opinions, I chose to run a message mapping interactive workshop. It wasn't something I'd done before, but I thought that showing how Content Design worked would not only educate the team, but expose the complexity of this content problem. **(Task)**

Before the workshop, I took all the messages we needed to convey in the product and put them into a FigJam board, each on its own sticky. I then created a linear map of the product for the team to place the messages. Each person: PM, PMM, Design and Research got to do their own version. In the end, we looked for patterns together, resolved different takes on the exercise, and ended up with an agreed-upon direction that would inform the in-product content. **(Action)**

The workshop meant I had an easier time not only executing the Content Design, but getting buy-in on my choices. After all, the team had helped make the decisions. This led to fewer revisions on the content than expected, which allowed me to finalize the

content earlier than planned. It also raised the team's collective trust and understanding of Content Design as a discipline and me, specifically as a practitioner. **(Result)**

One story, but it can answer so many questions, such as:

Tell me about a time you took initiative (or)
Tell me about a time you addressed a tricky content problem (or)
Tell me about a time you worked on something totally new (or)
Tell me about a time you drove collaboration (etc).

So, now it's your turn

Beyond setting up your case studies, this is the biggest chunk of work you'll do. But I promise you, it's worth it. Take some time to answer, using the STAR format, some very typical interview questions. This is you, building your story bank. Remember, most of these stories will be able to work for more than one kind of question, so your effort now can have lasting impact throughout all of your interviews. Set up a doc for yourself, where you're building your answers to the following questions:

- What is the work you're most proud of?
- What's something you've geeked out about?
- Tell me about a mistake you made. How did you overcome it?
- Tell me about a time you had to handle difficult feedback.
- Tell me about a time you disagreed with someone on your team.
- Tell me about a time you developed a process or new system.
- Tell me about a time you used research to make a decision.

For each of these, go through the work:

Situation (10%)

Task (20%)

Action (50%)

Result (20%)

At the end, you'll have a bank of stories you can likely draw from for the rest of your career (though you'll want to update the bank with new stories as your experience grows!).

Write your own questions too

While naturally the conversation is going to be focused on you and what you bring to the table, the more genuinely interested and curious you are about your interviewer, the role, and the company, the better off you'll be. Why? Way to be curious already!

Interviewing the interviewer

There aren't a lot of "automatically disqualified" things you can do in an interview. I've hired people who were a little late, who had to reschedule a few times, who didn't have perfect portfolios or resumes. But if your answer to "Do you have any questions for me?" is "nope," then I think that might be the end of the line for you.

I'm not being a jerk here, and I'm not standing on ceremony or etiquette. Not having any questions means you're lacking core curiosity or interest that's crucial to UX work. I'm not alone here.

> "What gives me pause is when someone has no questions at all. Good designers are inquisitive by nature. They want to

> understand the big, messy problems. So if a candidate says 'Nope. I'm good,' it signals to me a lack of curiosity – and that makes me question how engaged they'll be in the work."
> –Andy Welfle, co-author of *Writing is Designing*

Your questions do a few really crucial things for you in the interview process:

They get you the information you need in order to make an informed decision if this is the right job for you.

They demonstrate to your interviewer a genuine curiosity and interest in the role, the manager, or the company.

They keep the conversation going.

So, what are you going to ask? There's a few ways to go:

Generic questions about the job, the role, the company.
Mostly these logistical things should be covered in the job description, a careers page, or the recruiting interview. There's no harm in asking them, but is this really the information you need? Also, they're not going to lead to the most interesting discussion, and might solicit some pretty generic responses. Boring questions in, boring responses out.

These might look like:

- What are the working hours?
- What's the company culture like?
- What's work/life balance like?
- Is payment on an every other week or bi-weekly cadence?
- What are the perks?

Tactical questions for the hiring manager.

This isn't to say fact-based questions aren't out of the...question. There are some really important things you should ask based on your past experience, what you're looking for in a role, and in a team structure. These are things that may not be wholly apparent from the research you were able to do so far, or even go beyond the recruiters expertise. Ask away! These might look like:

- What's the ratio between Content Designers and Product Designers?
- What's the reporting structure in the Design org?
- What kind of tools do you use to do the job?
- What are some of your team ceremonies?
- How many direct reports do you have?
- What's your management philosophy?
- What kind of growth do you envision for this role?
- What risks are posed by this role remaining open?

Philosophical questions you can ask anyone.

Keep these questions in your pocket that you can ask anyone, anytime. These are some open-ended, role-agnostic questions that not only show interest in role and in the company, but in the person you're interviewing with. They're deceptively simple in their structure, and can elicit some of the most revealing answers. Not that you want to put your interviewer on the back foot or make them feel uncomfortable, but these are the kinds of questions that don't always get asked.

- What motivates you?
- What keeps you up at night?
- What keeps you engaged in your role right now?
- What are you most excited about in the next year (for work or otherwise)?
- What are you most interested in learning about?
- What's the work you're most proud of?

This is the one question I hate: Is there anything about me that would keep me from successfully getting this job?

I've seen chatter on LinkedIn on why people love this question, but I find it manipulative and puts the interviewer on the spot. That really isn't the dynamic you're looking to cultivate. Beyond that, you're not going to get a useful answer: hiring decisions are made by committee, and the person you're asking may not have a full view of the role, the requirements, and all the conversations you've had so far. I'm not a fan.

An exercise in curiosity

The more you learn, the more you're able to make a decision if this job is right for you. The company isn't the only one making a decision here. Maybe you love the brand, but then the more you learn about the way the work works sours you on it. Or maybe it all looks exceptional on paper, but you don't vibe with the team or the hiring manager. Or maybe the company and the team is right, but the very specific job you're applying for doesn't match your particular strengths or values. There are a lot of reasons a role might not be a good fit, and it's on you as an equal and interested part of the process to make that assessment.

And yes, you're also still trying to make a good impression. The best way to do this is to be genuinely curious, to ask questions that get you the information you need, and to get the interviewer talking and engaged. Asking the right questions will unlock their excitement and give you a good idea as to what makes them tick. Get them talking and engaged, and they'll walk away with a very good impression of you.

Also, secret tip: it's ok to ask the same question to different people. Might be interesting to compare and contrast their answers!

Do just enough research

Heading into an interview, you want to be informed about the company, without coming off as a stalker. You want to do enough digging to show your enthusiasm for the role and the work, but not so much that you put people off. Keep it professional, not personal.

Find out who you're interviewing with, then do a light LinkedIn look-up

Finding out someone's title, general job description and experience is great. Just so you know who you're talking to. And even if you do go really deep, try not to make it weird. Just because you found you went to the same college, maybe don't show up wearing your alma mater's sweatshirt. I've had people switch to Russian in an interview with me because they saw that's what I studied in college. Keep cool, and stay relevant. And don't stalk their Instagram.

Check out recent company news

Educate yourself with headlines, blog posts, or social media happenings. Check out their LinkedIn page. You want to see what's top of mind for employees (and avoid any obvious faux pas). For example, if Netflix just announced an entirely new reality sports division, you might not want to ask, "Has Netflix ever thought about getting into the reality sports game?" Do a little homework, save yourself some awkwardness.

Check out the competition as well

Expand your search to see what their competitors are up to, especially if you have a sense of what part of the business you might be working on. Not only might you find some interesting information, you'll continue to show up as curious, informed, and genuinely invested in the role to which you're applying.

Preparing your presentation

Beyond that resume that got you in the door, your presentation deck is the most important job-search artifact you'll put together. End-to-end, this is where you're really telling your story (and not just your case studies). It's a big undertaking, but it's the best way to show and tell what you're all about.

> "There is no part of your presentation that isn't considered part of your portfolio: your preamble about who you are, your background, the places you've worked: that's all your portfolio too. You can't just start with a bunch of facts, and then switch gears to 'ok, now let's look at my portfolio.' You'll lose your audience. The details about you shouldn't be tacked on at the beginning. It all comes together to tell your story. I might start out by saying 'I really got into Content Design when I read Richard Scarry as a kid, let me show you how.'
> -Chelsea Larsson, Content Design Leader

While it's a bit of work to put together, the good news is, one deck can work for many interviews (just make sure you change the cover page to reflect the right company and date!). There are about a million and a half templates for portfolio presentations on the internet (and in Figma), and there's no shame in adapting them (especially if graphic design is not your passion).

Here are the key points you'll want to hit:

A little intro about you
2-3 slides max. This is where you tell your story: maybe where you're from, how you got here. Your relevant experience along the way. Every single piece of this is teeing up why the job you're

applying for is the next, obvious step in your career. You can set this up from both a personal and professional perspective.

For example, for a consumer-facing content role, focusing on Safety at Lyft, I might show:

Professional: copywriter at XYZ companies → Content Designer at XYZ companies, always focusing on Integrity and User Safety.

Personal: love exploring the city of SF (and the world) using all modes of transportation: bike, cars, walking.

You can tailor your intro to the job you're applying for: choosing to highlight or feature different aspects of your journey that are relevant to the role.

Consider a "career highlights" page

Reserve one slide to bullet out the things in your career that make you who you are. This might look like a feature you shipped, a company you worked with or for, something you learned, or something you taught. It's a nice, quick way to speak to key things about you, without going into excessive detail.

Your case studies

Next up, you'll want to format the case studies you're showing for presentation mode. This means choosing the case studies that are most relevant to the role and adapting them so that you're telling the story live (vs reading them on your site or in a leave-behind). This might look like a lot less text on the page (because you're speaking to it), and overall more simple slides that are illustrative of the story (vs. incredibly detailed eye charts that no one can read from the back of the room).

Be wary of "we"

While design is inherently a collaborative effort, talking a little too much about what "we" did isn't going to tell your story. It's a balance that needs to be struck. On one hand, you want to show what kind of work you like to do, and the impact you've made. On the other hand, you don't want to come off like you did the whole thing, soup-to-nuts.

> "Hiding your role in a successful operation makes you look disingenuous and ineffectual and – ironically – even more arrogant because you appear to be taking personal credit for a group's work. The interviewer you asked you to tell her about a time that you led a team, after all, and here you are talking about what everyone else did...
>
> Speak to your accomplishments, what you did and what was important to you. This isn't bragging, it's being upfront about what drives you and the kind of problems you're keen to solve."
>
> -Angela Guido, *Interview Hero*

> "Be very clear about what was your contribution and what was the team's contribution. Make sure not to over-index on the 'I', because it seems like you're not a collaborator, but then too much into the 'we' because then the panel doesn't know what you contributed."
>
> -Christina (Maz) Mazurowski, Product Recruitment, Datadog

Rehearse, rehearse, relax

When it comes to your presentation, you want to be well-rehearsed, but not overly so. Work from notes if you need them, but try to avoid reading a word-by-word script. The whole point of the presentation is to make a genuine connection with the audience, and reading from a script really puts a barrier between you and them. Also, slow down.

Your nerves are going to make you go a lot faster than you think. You don't want to skip over the details. Go slower than you think you need to. You got this. You'll do great. Make sure to rehearse for time too.

> "I can think of at least two interviews at Meta where candidates ran out of time white presenting their portfolios. It may be one thing if these were interviews for junior, early career roles, but these were for senior manager positions. The crappy thing about the interview experience is it's a brief moment in time where a candidate and interviewer can 'get a look at each other' to make decisions that will have long-term implications. Unfortunately, for both of these candidates, the fact that they ran out of time in their presentation was a big knock against them during the interview debrief and neither ended up getting the roles."
> -Joel Solomon, Content Design Manager

Rehearse a bit, keep it conversational, and try to relax as best as you can. You're going to do great.

The design exercise dilemma

Once the biggest drag in interviewing as a Designer, the design exercise is slowly losing favor, but it's still out there. A design exercise might be something that you take home and do independently, or you might do it right there on the spot. There are often parameters given: only spend one hour, show your thinking, use any resources you find on the internet. For some people, they are a deal-breaker on if they want to apply for a certain company.

- Why they are problematic:
  They are often unfair: for take-home work, people may definitely

spend more than the given time, which gives them an advantage over those who don't have the time to spare. The work is quite uninformed and not how design works: you aren't given the opportunity to ask questions or understand the full context of the work. There is a commonly-held belief that the candidate is being asked to do "free work," or that the output of the exercise will end up being shipped. I have to think that's a bit of a conspiracy, and if that has happened anecdotally, it's likely a result of two designers coming to the same conclusion (a designer who works in the company and the candidate).

- Why they can be useful:
  Doing these design exercises might give you insight into the company and how it works. The way they set up the problem, the parameters they give, and the work they want to show. It's rare that you get to have a behind-the-scenes look, and a design exercise might reveal something to you. Also, it gives you a clear idea of the kind of work you'd be doing. Sometimes, they can even be fun (I know, again, I have a weird idea of fun).

For Dave Hoffer, a design leader, a design exercise and the process around it exposed a lot about the company he was interviewing for and gave him a sense of how they functioned (as well as their dysfunction).

> "I was interviewing at a small organization, a consultancy. Generally, they did very little design, but they were looking to me to bring a certain level of design leadership and credibility to their org. I would have been there to design, yes, but also to win work.
>
> I talked to the founder and had a great conversation. I met more of the leaders across the org, and every conversation was incredible. Really interesting work, interesting people.

> Finally, they said, 'We'd like you to do a design test.'
>
> I agreed, but asked them what the rubric was for gauging it, what would I be evaluated on. What skills were they looking to assess. They didn't give me much of a response, but I decided to go ahead with it.
>
> On the day of the test, I got on a call with the junior designers they had, and they sent me a design brief. I did what I would have done in a real-world scenario: I asked a lot of questions. I asked about the user needs, about the constraints, about research. I started asking questions, and I kept asking questions.
>
> I didn't get the job.
>
> In the debrief, I asked them what had happened, and they said it was the test. They were expecting me to open up Figma, to make screens. But that isn't how design works."
>
> -Dave Hoffer, Design Leader

If you're feeling uncomfortable about a design exercise
You might ask if it can be a paid exercise, or if there's another way you might demonstrate what they're looking for. When I was interviewing at a small start-up to be their first Content Designer, they proposed an exercise. My first question was who was going to be reviewing it: a Content Designer or someone else. When it turned out it was going to be the Design lead and the CEO, neither of whom had had content experience before, I asked if it would be possible to do the exercise live: this meant I could walk them through my thinking, show how Content Design could be more collaborative, and meant I didn't have to work in a vacuum. It worked.

This kind of negotiation may not be possible at a big, huge company. Sometimes the design exercise is just part of the process.

Takeaways

Build your story

Having a cache of stories to draw on means you're ready to answer many of the most common behavioral questions

Do just enough research

Be well-informed about the company, its direction, and the people you're meeting with. Stop short of being creepy.

Prepare, prepare, relax

Summon your confidence and the things you're genuinely excited about. That's what'll come through.

CHAPTER SIX

It's interview go-time

First things first, take the concept of an "interview" out of your mind. Poof, let it go. Instead, reframe the interaction you're about to have as a two-way conversation. While yes, it's an important one and yes, the focus is a bit more on you than the person you're speaking with, but don't assume it's going to be an interrogation. Instead, think about the person you're speaking with, about the information you need to get, and about how the interviewer feels.

A little empathy, all the preparation you've already done, and a good dose of interview etiquette and you'll be on your way to the next round of interviews. Er, conversations.

Be honest, be curious, and, know when to STFU.

Prepare your day around your interview

Interviews are intense, even if you're a weirdo like me who genuinely enjoys them. Depending on the scope and stakes of the interview, I'll still find time to mentally (and sometimes physically) prepare, so my head is in the right space before I start introducing myself.

Eat, hydrate, exercise

This is not a checklist. These are just a few of the pre-gaming things I might do in anticipation of any big event, but especially an interview. These intense/interesting conversations can be really draining, and there's little worse than feeling your blood sugar start to tank and your performance flagging. In long-distance cycling, we talk a lot about bonking, where your glycogen stores drop and suddenly your legs decide they have opted out of the ride. It. Is. The. Worst. You don't want to bonk on the road, and you definitely don't want to bonk in an interview. Get a snack. Plop an electrolytes tablet in your water bottle. Go for a walk. Inhale, exhale, repeat.

Make the time (and maybe make some tea)

We are an over-scheduled people. From wake to sleep, Monday-Sunday, many of us are just trying to do too much. Context switching is exhausting, and adds a little tax and friction to your cognition. If you can, find a little window to settle and clear your head before you walk in the door or launch the meeting. Choose a transitional activity, like taking a walk, taking a 5-minute breathing meditation, or just making a cup of tea can chill you out before start. No matter if you're there in person or taking the call from home, see if you can find a few minutes to just sit outside and breathe. No phone, no scrolling.

Wear what you need to feel confident

If I was out clothes shopping with my mother as a high school or college student, all I had to do was put on a blazer, and she would beam with pride. "Dress for the job you want," she'd chime immediately, reaching for the garment so she could buy it for me for any upcoming interview. I would wear it to the interview, awkwardly shifting under the shoulder pads and futzing with the buttons until I got home to wrest it off, throw it in the back of my closet, and hope it was enough to get the job. And as far as the job I wanted? I don't think I ever saw a copywriter wearing a blazer in earnest. It just wasn't a thing we did.

After awhile, I stopped putting on interview blazers. I kept getting jobs. I found clothes that were more suited to me (pun intended!) and to the industry.

You don't have to wear a blazer to get the job. But you should find whatever it is in your closet that makes you feel comfortable and confident and the best version of your professional self.

A little interview etiquette

Let's get some basics out of the way. These are the littlest things you can do to make a good impression. Like you might for a first date. It's not just about ticking the boxes or about being old-fashioned, etiquette is about making people feel comfortable and respected. When you're showing up for an interview, people are expecting to see the very best version of yourself, and the little missteps are going to be viewed globally and catastrophically. "If they can't show up to this call on time, why would I think they would be able to hit a deadline?" So do yourself a favor and get easy stuff out of the way and make an excellent impression from the start.

Early is on time

My mom once had a friend who was always late, whenever they made plans. Every time, without fail. It pissed her off, and she finally spoke to her about it. "When you're late, it tells me that your time is more valuable than mine." Damn, mom. Good insight! Her friend got it, never forgot it, and wasn't late to meet my mom again.

Same rules here. There will be plenty of time in your career where your time is more important than someone else's. This isn't one of them.

Just like before you arrived at the interview, find a little bit of breathing room. Even if you're the only person in the virtual room, sit and settle into the mental space, take a sip of water, and be ready to be present. This way you're not rushing to fix your hair or find a pen just as your interviewer is joining the chat. Find calm in these few minutes. You've got this.

Listen actively

Part of making a good impression and really connecting with another human being is making sure they feel heard and comfortable. The best way to do this is by being present and meeting their gaze. Most of us do this instinctively, naturally. We hear the tone in someone's voice, and our expression modulates to meet their mood. Standard-issue empathy.

When your interviewer is speaking, be open and interested and really, really listen. Whatever they're saying is full of crucial clues about what they hold important. These are all things you'll likely want to use to frame answers to their questions.

A note about interviewing online:

- **Cheat eye contact.** When having a conversation you'll want to look at your interviewer's face, because that's what we do, natu-

rally. Instead, try and look at the camera on your computer (stare at the little green dot!), since on their end, it will look as if you're matching their gaze and looking into their eyes.

- **Ignore your dumb, beautiful face.** Most video apps let you minimize your own frame. Do it before the session starts so you won't be distracted by yourself. If you're concerned with your stage presence, record yourself with a friend and review the video on your own time. This isn't the right time to be glancing at your own face.
- **Position frames strategically.** Reduce the size of the video window and move it towards the top of the screen, near the camera. That brings your focus closer to the camera when you're looking at your conversation partner and improves the perception of attention.

You are the solution they're looking for

Now that we've got the etiquette stuff out of the way, let's get to the other way you're going to show up: your attitude. Yes, an interview is absolutely about a crucial exchange of information: "are you right for the job, and is the company right for you?" There will be questions, there will be answers. Standard protocol.

Just as we framed your resume as a narrative, the next chapter in the story being the job you're applying for, think about framing yourself in a particular way in relationship to the company. They have a problem (an open position) and you are the solution.

This isn't about why you want this job.
This isn't about what you want in your career trajectory.
This is about how you are the solution.

Be the lid to their pot

In your pre-interview preparations, you should have been piecing together the problem they're trying to solve. You may have gathered the information from the job posting, from your recruiter interview, from blog posts or any other research you'd done. By now, you should have a good idea of the problem they're trying to solve, either from the areas you suspect they're growing, or expertise gaps on the team they're seeking to fill.

That's where you come in.

Think about framing all your answers as you being the solution to the problem, and why your approach, your experience, your expertise, your strengths are all perfectly matched to the gap.

For example, say you're meeting with a hiring manager on the design team. Based on your conversations, you understand that this role is focused on ecommerce, with near-term priorities involving internationalization. You found this out by closely reading the job description, which gave you some of these clues, as well as your initial chat with the recruiter. The hiring manager asks you a pretty broad question: "Tell me about your career path in design."

Now's your chance. Which of these sounds more appealing to you as a listener?

Option 1:
Your career path in design, as if you were reading your CV to someone.

Option 2:
Your career path in design, omitting granular details, highlighting aspects relevant to ecommerce and internationalization experience,

and conveying an arc that ultimately lands at this role. Your answers should not be generic, but instead tailored to the specific role you're interviewing for.

Interviewing is an exercise in sales

Once I had an opening for a short-term contract role. I needed an expert to come in, execute some work, and leave the place better than they found it. (Not how I usually like to run a team, but I was in a jam – but that's a story for the other side of this book, that you're also going to read, right? Right!).

This was all in the job description: short-term, quick onboarding, keep things from unraveling, thank you, please come again.

A friend of a friend was looking for some contract work. He came highly recommended and so I set aside some time to talk with him for the role. Instead of coming in to talk about the problem I was trying to solve, he focused on what he needed and what he was looking for in his career. Why he was looking to learn more on the job about UX and wanted to find a new home on a Content Design team. His background was erratic and he focused more on his gaps and what he wanted to learn, rather than what he could do for the business.

What I wanted to hear was how he had made a big impact at other short-term gigs in the past (because there were a few of these on his resume), how he was a sponge for information, and how he had successfully onboarded quickly in complex spaces. What I heard instead was what he needed, what he wanted, and frankly, it sounded like it was going to be a lot of work for me. Because he was a friend of a friend, I felt bad turning him down (and I did have a follow-up chat with him after to give some interviewing advice).

Interviewing is an exercise in sales, and the best people in sales don't

come off as salesmen. It's not about "what do I need to do to get you in a car today?" Great salesmen really believe in their product, not just about closing the deal. When you're interviewing, you're the product. Having a clear understanding of your values, of your strengths, and what makes you the perfect match for their needs will lead to a more successful, more engaging conversation.

Be honest, but tactful

Beyond the little bit of research you did on who is interviewing you, you aren't going to know anything and everything about who you're chatting with and what they've worked on. As a designer, you're going to be asked for your opinion, your perspective, what you might improve or what trade-offs you might make. And how you respond will show your skills, your experience, your design philosophy and how you solve problems. What you don't want to do is put your foot in your mouth or come off as cynical.

> "A candidate began sharing her screen with a sample piece of content and said 'I'd redo all this. It just doesn't make sense. Honestly whoever wrote it should be fired.' I asked her to elaborate on how she would improve it, what was wrong with it, etc, and she just said 'It's bad.'
>
> She didn't know, but I was the one who wrote that particular article. 😬 The rest of the interview was just as painful, and I'll never get that moment out of my mind. Me trying to nod along and encourage a discussion while she continued scrolling while presenting her screen and just saying things like 'this section sucks. This is dumb.' etc."
>
> –Chase Bucklew-Geddes, Content Operations Lead

Eek. In my experience I've seen cynicism sneak in about all kinds of

things: departments, product areas, AI, design in general. Even if you have these (often valid!) perspectives, interviewing is a time when you want to show your most productive, positive, and optimistic side. That doesn't mean all smiles and rainbows, but it does mean keeping some of the darker takes unsaid.

How shutting the fuck up can help you land a job

A friend of mine and I had been through the interview process for the same job at the same company. Neither of us got an offer. It was a weird experience for both of us, and one we debriefed about months later. We had gone through about a dozen 1:1 interviews, all of them structured differently.

"Did you talk to that one design director? The British guy who was kinda in a rush?"

"Oh! Yes! I remember him. He talked the whole time. Didn't ask me a single question."

"Exactly. I remember thinking, 'The way I'm going to ace this interview is by saying 'oh, that's really interesting,' whenever he pauses to take a break."

"100%!"

Even though neither of us got the job, we had had the exact same experience and felt confident, every step of the way. Sometimes, you just need to STFU.

But Margo, what could you possibly mean? How can I not talk the entire time I'm being interviewed, it's all about me, isn't it? No, so

much no. Functionally, there are two speeds in any given interview: the part where you talk, and the part where they talk. Keep in mind which part you're in, and act accordingly.

We've talked about the part where you talk: centering your answers around being the solution, asking insightful questions that express genuine curiosity. Now there's the part where they talk.

Here are the rules:

STFU.
Seriously. Don't say a damn thing. Listen. Listen actively. Nod encouragingly. Take in what they're saying and use that to inform the questions you might have or the answers you might give. Take notes if you need to.

Do. Not. Interrupt.
You might get super inspired by a thing the interviewer is saying. You may want to add in your experience or ideas. You're excited about how this is going, and you are sure you already know where the end of their sentence is going. Stop it. No. Being interrupted feels really, really shitty. This is not how you want to have an interviewer leave an interview feeling. I've seen it in the "cons" column of interviewer notes time and time again. "Interrupted me a lot." Just don't do it. People like being listened to, they don't like being interrupted.
If it helps, focus on the sensation of your lips being closed. I'm serious. It can help. Wait your turn.

Enjoy the free time
In any given interview, you're going to talk sometimes, and the interviewer is going to talk sometimes. Obviously, it's a bit more stressful when you're in the hot seat. Maybe you're acutely aware of the words coming out of your mouth, or the interviewer's reaction to it, or if

you're making any sense at all. It's the more difficult part. But, there's the part where the interviewer is talking. Where your only job is to listen intently, nod and smile, and pick up any important clues about the job. Interviewer-talking time is free time, so don't take it away from yourself.

Takeaways

Practice good interview etiquette
Be on time. Be prepared. Be your very best self. As the very old commercial says, you never get a second chance to make a first impression.

Sell yourself as a solution
Match your experience to their needs, your background to their requirements. This isn't (just) about why this job is good for you, it's about how you can help them.

Wait your turn to talk
Don't interrupt, no matter how excited you are to jump into the conversation. Being heard feels great, being interrupted does not.

CHAPTER SEVEN

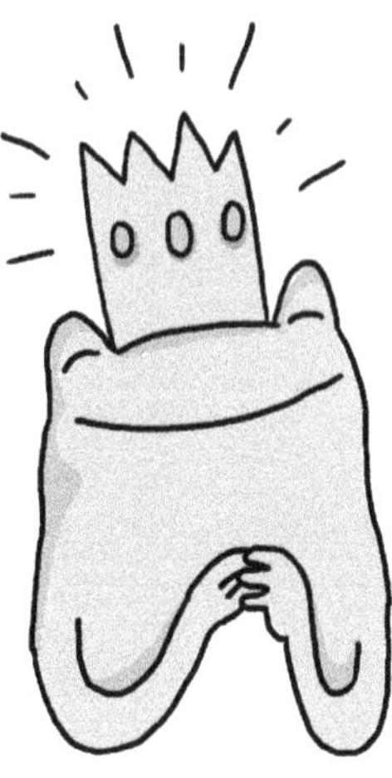

After the interview: knowing your worth through offers (and otherwise)

Hot damn you made it through the gauntlet of interviews. Well done. That was a lot. So now let's get into what happens after it's all done: getting an offer, getting a no, or (gulp) getting ghosted.

After the interview: gratitude and patience

You just did so much work. You researched, you rehearsed. You got all your stories set and you told them like a pro. You asked great questions and listened intently to the answers. Getting a job is a lot of work. But now it's time to take a little break. Take the foot off the gas. The ball is in their court and no amount of ruminating and fretting is going to make the wheels of hiring move faster. So do what you can do, and then chill. Here's what your timeline looks like:

Within 24 hours: send a thank-you note

While the last interview is still fresh in your mind, send a personalized thank-you note to the recruiter, and ask them to pass your thanks around to the rest of the team. You don't need to hit up each individual you spoke with. Highlight what you enjoyed through the interview process, what you learned, and why you're interested in the role. Keep it short. Keep it specific.

Example:

Dear Friendly Recruiter,

Just wanted to drop you a quick note to thank you for the opportunity to interview with Gamma Corp. I genuinely enjoyed my conversations with Raj, Tina, and Albert. Speaking with them, I learned even more about cathode ray-guns and would love the opportunity to bring my experience with package design to complement their exciting work. Do let me know if there's anything else I can answer, and I hope to hear from you soon.

That's it. You've done everything you need to do. Go outside. Go get a nice cup of tea. Touch grass.

Within 1-2 weeks: follow up

No response to the thank-you note? Radio silence? This is where it doesn't begin to feel good. But not all hope is lost. Any number of things could be happening that have exactly nothing to do with you: they're still talking to other candidates, someone on the hiring committee has gone on vacation or had a family emergency, some work suddenly became very urgent. You must chill. That said, following up again within this time is totally reasonable. Keep it short, keep it neutral in tone.

Example:

Dear Friendly Recruiter,

Hope all is well in your world. Just wanted to check back in on the cathode ray-gun package design role, as I haven't heard back from you yet. I'm still genuinely excited about the prospect and hope to hear back from you soon either way.

Now you've for sure done all you can do! It's either gonna go one of three ways: you get a no, you get an offer, or you get ghosted. Let's talk about the worst one first:

Getting ghosted sucks

> "You can't control others, but you can control how you respond to the sound of silence. That's where you power is. If you still don't hear back after reaching out, feel good knowing that you followed up in a professional manner."
> -Gretta Perlmutter, host of "Coping with Ghosting" podcast

While getting a 'no' is a pretty bad outcome, I'd argue getting ghosted

is worse. All that work, all that energy, just to have it dissipate into the ether. No feedback, no resolution. But it happens.

And it absolutely shouldn't.

In researching this book, I dug into ghosting to try and understand why it happens: could there be any justifiable reason to let a candidate drift away without a decision either way? Maybe there was a legal risk to not continue a conversation. Maybe a candidate started acting inappropriately. But I couldn't find anything. Universally, it's agreed that it's a bad practice. A bad practice that still happens.

Ghosting is probably an indication about the health and organization of the company itself. Disorganization, indecision, or just crappy management. Sure, there might have been real reasons why the job went away: hiring a different candidate, budget cuts, an internal can didate, a shift of priorities. Maybe there were too many candidates or the recruiter just didn't want to deliver bad news. None of these reasons justify treating you badly. Makes me mad just thinking about it. So what can you do?

You have to just move on. You can set a deadline for yourself for how much you'll care about it, and once that time is past, it's over. You have a finite amount of time and energy, and it's best not spent after people that don't care about you.

I'm sorry. It shouldn't happen.

Dealing with 'no'

The good news is, you didn't get ghosted. The bad news is, they passed on you. And it stings every time. The most talented, qualified, kick-ass

candidates get rejected. It's happened to all of us. While getting the offer isn't in your control, how you react, respond, and move on is.

> "Sometimes a great candidate is not good for right now, or not good for what the company needs. Those are the hardest ones to turn down. At my company now, I need someone who can really wear so many hats, who can move super fast. If someone is used to working at the pace of shipping one thing a quarter, they're not going to fit. We're shipping every two weeks."
> -Chelsea Larsson, Content Design Lead

Accept 'no' with grace

It might be an email, it might be a phone call. You can hear it in their voice, or maybe get the message from the first word. "Unfortunately" is usually the tell. So what do you do? You take a deep breath, you accept the outcome and you respond calmly. There's no room for negotiation, for bargaining. Assume they didn't come to this decision lightly, or without sufficient consideration.

Reply with careful consideration

While you're under no obligation to reply, it might be a good idea to respond with some sort of acknowledgment of receipt. Write your own conclusion, and then you get to move on. You can also mention keeping the door open, just in case there's something else in the future.

Thank you for letting me know. While this outcome is definitely not what I had hoped for, I'm thankful for the experience and opportunity. If there's another role in the future at Gamma-Corp you feel might be a fit for me, I'd love to chat again.

Decide if you want the feedback

Some companies might offer you feedback on the interview, and why

they passed on you. It's entirely up to you if you feel up to hearing it. While of course, it's useful to get insight into your performance, rejection is emotionally fraught, and you may not be in the headspace to hear it. If you can ask for it in an email, then you can wait to open it until you're in the right mindset.

Move on

Just like with getting ghosted, getting a no is an emotional drain. Summon some resiliency. Get distracted. Do something else. This doesn't mean you should jump right back into the LinkedIn pool. You might need a minute to recover before you're really ready to put yourself back out there.

Because you're gonna keep going, and one day, you're going to get a big YES. Let's talk about that exciting day, shall we?

Fuck yeah, you got an offer. Let's negotiate.

Negotiating is about more than money

First, let's talk about why you should negotiate (besides the obvious). You're not being greedy. They're not going to take the offer away. They're expecting you to negotiate. And you should, because you're not just negotiating for you.

- **Negotiating raises the salary bar for your industry.** If everyone accepted lower salaries, then the average salary for your role/ your level/your industry is lower. When you negotiate for a higher salary, you are setting the average higher. This benefits everyone.

- **Giving yourself a raise.** Outside of a promotion, this is the only time you have to really see your salary move up in a meaningful

way. Cost-of-living increases may come, merit increases also. But neither of these are sure things. This is the time where you have the power to advocate for yourself.

- **Practice for other negotiations.** Outside of being a lawyer, negotiation isn't a regular part of our jobs. It is a skill, and it takes practice. Opting out of negotiation means taking away one of these few opportunities to give it a shot. Go on, try it out. You might like what you end up with.

The salary offer is a starting point

At some point in your recruiter conversations or early screening, you would have given your salary expectations. We talked about that a bit in Chapter 5. The salary you get in your offer shouldn't be too far from that, and shouldn't come as a surprise. No matter if the number is higher, lower, or exactly what you asked for, know that it's a starting point. It's already been budgeted that you're going to negotiate, and you not negotiating is leaving your own money on the table.

Salaries are often calculated in a "band," which means for your role at your level, there's a range you're in until you get a promotion to the next level. Offers are going to come in at the low or middle range of the band, to give you room to get merit increases without going out of the bounds of the band. Frankly, that math is not your problem and future merit increases are for future you. What this does mean for you now is that there is an upper limit you can hit, and your goal is to try and get to the middle or higher end of the band.

Whatever happens: **do not accept the first offer right away**. Time is on your side. Receive the offer, say thank you, convey that you're super excited about the role and the opportunity, then ask when they need a decision by. That's to buy you some time to think about what to do next.

If the offer comes in high (or what you asked for): Nice! Love that. Good feeling. Still negotiate. There's room in the band, and you're not being greedy by negotiating for more. No one will judge you. Put the extra in savings. It's fine.

If the offer comes in very low: If the offer comes in way lower than your stated salary requirements, then you should have a frank chat with your recruiter. Even though you haven't signed, you have a bit of leverage here. They want you, they're excited about you, and they need to make it worth it to you. If you're super excited about the job/role/potential impact, and your budget and life can make it work, then maybe it is worth it to take a lower salary. But you'll still negotiate, and maybe go a little extra on negotiating for non-salary compensation.

Ok, I'm ready to negotiate, tell me what to say

Worried about fucking this whole thing up? Not sure how you can justify asking for more in this economy? Good news, the fewer words you say in negotiation the better. While talking is hard, not talking can be even harder. You have to focus, you have to practice, you have to ask for what you want, and then STFU.

And it doesn't have to happen live. Taylor Howard, a Principal Content Designer at Cash app offered this incredible advice:

"I do not like to negotiate on the phone. I feel more comfortable writing something." I'll say, "I'll send you a note later with my thoughts." Then later I'll write, "This is what you offered. Can we get closer to this number."

So smart!

But, even if you do want to make it a phone call, there's a simple pattern you can use. It works either way. Here's the formula:

1. Restate your enthusiasm for the role. This might include details about the company, the people you met with, or the area you'll be working in.
2. Ask for more
3. STOP TALKING

You don't need to justify. You don't need to explain. Asking for what you want can be a complete sentence. It might look like this:

You: "Andrew, thanks so much for the offer. I am really looking forward to working with the unicorns at KittyPonyClub. I had an incredible time getting to know all the people and magical creatures I'd be working with. In terms of salary, I was hoping to get closer to $150,000."

...

Silence

No talk.

Focus on the sensation of your lips being pressed together.

Don't speak.

The recruiter (or hiring manager, or your other point-of-contact) then will get very business-like and may say something like: "We're already at the top of the band," or "this is the going salary for this role and this rate." They also will probably say something like, "Let me go back to the team and see what I can do."

(now it's ok for you to talk again).

You: "Thanks so much! I look forward to next steps."

/end of scary negotiations

What else is on the proverbial table

From here, you may go back and forth another round, but usually the first big effort is where you'll get the most change. If they come back with no more money to offer, then you may want to ask about other possible perks/benefits/compensation, but only if they're worth it to do the negotiation for you.

- Sign-on bonus
  If one wasn't offered at the start, see if there's one out there. This also might come in the form of equity. If it's based on equity, make sure to understand the vesting schedule. If it's a 10% bonus that vests over four years, it really isn't much of a bonus!

- Stock/equity/options
  This also may have been a part of your initial offer. See if there isn't more room in the grant. Keep in mind that stock (and its various incarnations) is usually later money, not now money. It won't impact your month-to-month budget and won't offset a low salary in the immediate sense.

- Vacation
  I don't know about this one, to be honest. It's often listed as a negotiable, but mostly it's set by a company policy based on tenure.

- Start date
  This won't earn you any money, but it can find you some peace of mind. If you're working at a current job, need to give two weeks

notice, and then are thinking about starting the new job the following Monday, see if you can't buy yourself some time. Yes, this role has been open for a bit and they're eager to get you to work, but their emergency is not your emergency. If you can find yourself a week off for a family visit, an adventure vacation, or just staying home watching Star Trek: The Next Generation and eating cold cereal, it's worth it for a little brain reset before it's work time again.

- Work parameters
  Do you want to work from home? Hybrid model? Four days a week? Away one Thursday morning a month so you can watch the symphony have open rehearsal (so specific!). Now is the time to see what you can do to make your work/life balance balanced.

- Company car? Equipment?
  When I got my first big advertising job, I remember my step-father encouraging me to ask for a company car. He'd worked in the business, but it had been a few decades. I said, "Oh, they want me to work now, not in 1957," and he did me the favor of laughing at my joke. But Gary had a point: there are often surprise perks out there. When I interviewed with GM in 2020, I was amused to see that a company car was on the list of perks. Makes sense for GM! So as you're negotiating, see what's available from the company itself.

In the end, your total compensation, which includes salary, bonuses, equity, vacation, perks, etc, should feel worth it to you. While your excitement about the new job is a great feeling, it won't last forever. Work will become work, and when it does, you want to make sure you're feeling fairly compensated for your labor.

Turning down an offer with grace

I had been interviewing with a large ecommerce platform for about six weeks. I had friends who worked there who seemed really happy. The Content Design team had a great reputation: they'd show up in conferences with interesting things to say, the behind-the-scenes chatter was good. They were fully remote, which worked for my lifestyle, and all the conversations I had with them went really well. I was not surprised when they came in with an offer, and the offer was very generous. Maybe life-changing generous.

But I turned down the job.

Why? How? Margo WTF.

I know. There were two roles available: one for Consumer Trust and Safety, the other for building tools for business. The Trust and Safety one was right up my alley: it aligned with my strengths, interests, and background. I could do well there. The other role sounded really boring to me. And I know me: I have a hard time summoning genuine enthusiasm to build tools, especially B2B things. In the course of the interview, the Trust and Safety role was filled, so I was being offered the B2B one. And even though the company, the people, and the team was the same, I knew I wouldn't be successful. The hiring team believed in me, but I had to be honest: this wasn't the job for me. So that is what I told the recruiter.

I told her how positive my experience was. I told her how much I was interested in the team and the company. I also told her I would refer people to her in the future.

Even though the job had a lot going for it, I wasn't the right fit. I ended up somewhere that was much more aligned with my passion and interests, and the day-to-day was a lot more interesting and exciting for me.

Trust your gut

If you've been through the interview process and at any point, you got a weird feeling, listen to it. Just as you're putting your very best face forward through interviewing, the company should be doing the same with you. What you see is what you get.

> "Once, late in the process, I got the major ick. It was a company I was really excited about. I'd gone through all the interviews and it was going well, but then I got to the hiring manager. They talked for 20 minutes, said things like, 'I'm sure you're aware of my work.' I wasn't. Despite the rest of my experience, I knew then I could never work for this person because they didn't ask me one damn question."
> -Chelsea Larsson, Content Design Leader

If you're not feeling it, you're not feeling it. Accepting a job offer is a big move, and you don't have to do it. You came into this entire process by defining your values, knowing your strengths, and being strategic and smart about what makes a good job for you. If there's a mismatch, you know it, and you have to be honest with yourself. It might be overwhelming and confusing in the moment, especially if you're daunted by starting again, but taking the wrong job will find you back in this position anyway. You're going to be ok.

Turning down an offer is a privilege

You may not have this privilege. You may have to take the job for all the reasons, and that makes all the sense in the world. But, if you are not in a dire situation, then consider giving yourself the grace of turning down an offer if it's not right. Turning down the wrong offer is just as important as accepting the right one.

Before your first day

The interviews are behind you. The negotiations are done. Your start date is set. You've given notice at your current job. So what do you do now?

I invite you to rest.

No matter if it's just the weekend before your start date or you've taken a little time off, find a chunk of time to do nothing. You've been working so hard, emotions have been running deep, and you're about to get very busy with the new job: meeting all the new people, getting oriented, finding out where the bathrooms are, and identifying your first work nemesis. It's a lot.

Before all that begins, put a little gas in your emotional tank. It doesn't have to be a big, lavish tropical vacation (but it could be!) and maybe shouldn't be a lot of the errands you feel like you *should* do. Consider:

- Sitting on a bench and watching the world go by
- Getting into nature (a hike, a paddle, a picnic)
- Going to the farmer's market and making a nice meal
- Hitting up your local museum
- Going to a mid-day movie
- Doing a tourist thing in your own town
- Buying a new plant

You've done a lot. Enjoy the break. You earned this. You earned it all.

Good job.

Takeaways

Move on from the unfortunate outcomes

Rejections and getting ghosted are shitty. Do your best not to dwell, but instead to be kind to yourself, find some sort of resolution, and move forward.

Turning down an offer is ok

It has to be a good fit for you, too. Don't let desperation inform a decision. The right thing will come along.

Celebrate your win

Getting a job is a job. When you accept a new job, make sure to take a minute to rest and reflect before your first day.